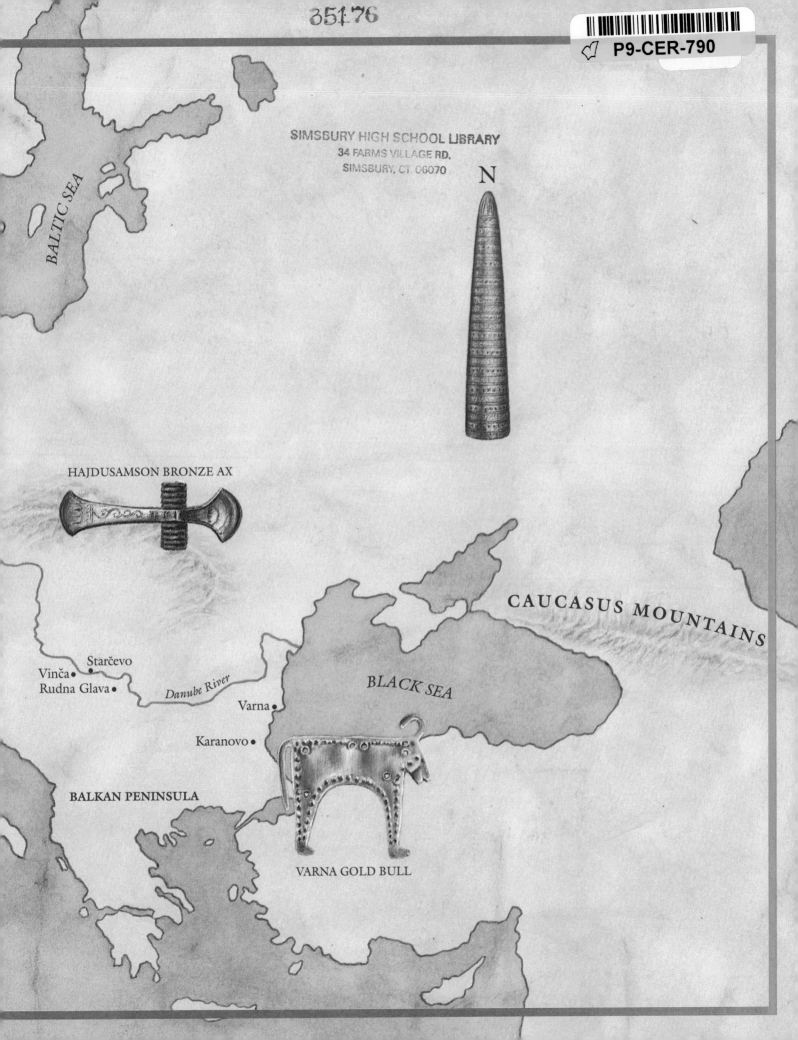

N

BALTIC SEA

HAJDUSAMSON BRONZE AX

CAUCASUS MOUNTAINS

Starčevo
Vinča
Rudna Glava
Danube River
Varna
BLACK SEA
Karanovo

BALKAN PENINSULA

VARNA GOLD BULL

TIME®
LIFE
BOOKS

Cover: The delicately carved lady of Brassempouy, from the foothills of the Pyrenees, is about 25,000 years old, making it one of the first depictions of a human face. The tiny ivory head—barely 1½ inches tall—is seen against the background of another work of early European art, a rock engraving of three snaking spirals from the ancient Irish tomb of Newgrange.

End paper: Painted by artist Paul Breeden on paper textured to look like hide the map shows important archaeological sites in prehistoric Europe. Representations of artifacts are shown near the location where they were discovered. Breeden also painted the images accompanying the timeline on pages 158 and 159.

EARLY EUROPE: MYSTERIES IN STONE

Time-Life Books is a division of Time Life Inc.

PRESIDENT and CEO: John M. Fahey Jr.

EDITOR-IN-CHIEF: John L. Papanek

TIME-LIFE BOOKS

MANAGING EDITOR: Roberta Conlan

Director of Design: Michael Hentges
Director of Editorial Operations: Ellen Robling
Director of Photography and Research: John Conrad Weiser
Senior Editors: Russell B. Adams Jr., Dale M. Brown, Janet Cave, Lee Hassig, Robert Somerville, Henry Woodhead
Special Projects Editor: Rita Thievon Mullin
Director of Technology: Eileen Bradley
Library: Louise D. Forstall

PRESIDENT: John D. Hall

Vice President, Director of Marketing: Nancy K. Jones
Vice President, Director of New Product Development: Neil Kagan
Vice President, Book Production: Marjann Caldwell
Production Manager: Marlene Zack
Quality Assurance Manager: James King

Library of Congress Cataloging in Publication Data
Early Europe: mysteries in stone / by the editors of Time-Life Books.
    p. cm. —(Lost civilizations)
Includes bibliographical references and index.
ISBN 0-8094-9100-1
    1. Man, Prehistoric—Europe.
    2. Megalithic monuments—Europe.
    3. Europe—Antiquities.
I. Time-Life Books. II. Series.
GN803.E27 1995   936—dc2094-46002
                              CIP

LOST CIVILIZATIONS

SERIES EDITOR: Dale M. Brown
Administrative Editor: Philip Brandt George

Editorial staff for *Early Europe: Mysteries in Stone*
Art Director: Ellen L. Pattisall
Picture Editor: Charlotte Marine Fullerton
Text Editors: Russell B. Adams Jr. (principal), Charlotte Anker, Robin Currie, Charles J. Hagner
Associate Editors/Research-Writing: Stephanie S. Henke, Jacqueline L. Shaffer
Senior Copyeditor: Barbara Fairchild Quarmby
Picture Coordinator: Catherine Parrott
Editorial Assistant: Patricia D. Whiteford

Special Contributors: Anthony Allan, Timothy Cooke, Cassandra Franklin-Barbajosa, Thomas Lewis, Barbara Mallen (text); Douglas J. Brown, Anna B. Gedrich, Maureen McHugh, Elizabeth Thompson, Ann-Louise Gates (research); Roy Nanovic (index).

Correspondents: Elisabeth Kraemer-Singh (Bonn), Christine Hinze (London), Christina Lieberman (New York), Maria Vincenza Aloisi (Paris), Ann Natanson (Rome). Valuable assistance was also provided by: Pavle Svabic (Belgrade), Angelika Lemmer (Bonn), Gay Kavanagh (Brussels), Barbara Gevene Hertz (Copenhagen), Judy Aspinall (London), Trini Bandres (Madrid), Saskia Van de Linde (Netherlands), Elizabeth Brown (New York), Dag Christensen (Oslo), Martha de la Cal (Portugal), Michal Donath (Prague), Leonora Dodsworth and Ann Wise (Rome), Dick Berry (Tokyo), Traudl Lessing (Vienna), Bogdan Turek (Warsaw).

The Consultants:

Christopher Chippindale is Senior Assistant Curator in the Cambridge University Museum of Archaeology and Anthropology and editor of the archaeological quarterly, *Antiquity*. In addition to having translated and edited Roger Joussaume's *Dolmens for the Dead*, a full survey of prehistoric European megaliths, he is author of the study *Stonehenge Complete*.

Victor H. Mair is professor of Chinese in the Department of Asian and Middle Eastern Studies at the University of Pennsylvania. While his main interests are Chinese lexicography and historical sociolinguistics, he has also been investigating Indo-European influences on the evolution of Chinese culture and has developed a special interest in the study of mummies in Xinjiang in Asia.

Sarunas Milisauskas specializes in Neolithic and Bronze Age Old World Archaeology, concentrating on settlement patterns, economics, and the origins of complex societies. Since 1965 he has conducted archaeological surveys and excavations of settlements in southeastern Poland. He is Professor of Anthropology at SUNY at Buffalo.

Erik Trinkaus is Professor of Anthropology at the University of New Mexico. A specialist in human osteology, anatomy, and Paleolithic Archaeology, he has been on excavations around the world. Author of numerous articles and critical reviews, he is coauthor with Pat Shipman of the seminal work *The Neandertals: Changing the Image of Mankind*.

Peter S. Wells, Professor of Anthropology at the University of Minnesota, specializes in European archaeology from the Paleolithic through the medieval period, focusing on trade, social structure, industry, and cultural change. He has participated in and directed numerous archaeological digs in Europe and is the author of numerous scholarly monographs and papers. Wells served as a consultant on *The Celts: Europe's People of Iron* in this same series.

This volume is one in a series that explores the worlds of the past, using the finds of archaeologists and other scientists to bring ancient peoples and their cultures vividly to life.

EARLY EUROPE: MYSTERIES IN STONE

By the Editors of Time-Life Books
TIME-LIFE BOOKS, ALEXANDRIA, VIRGINIA

CONTENTS

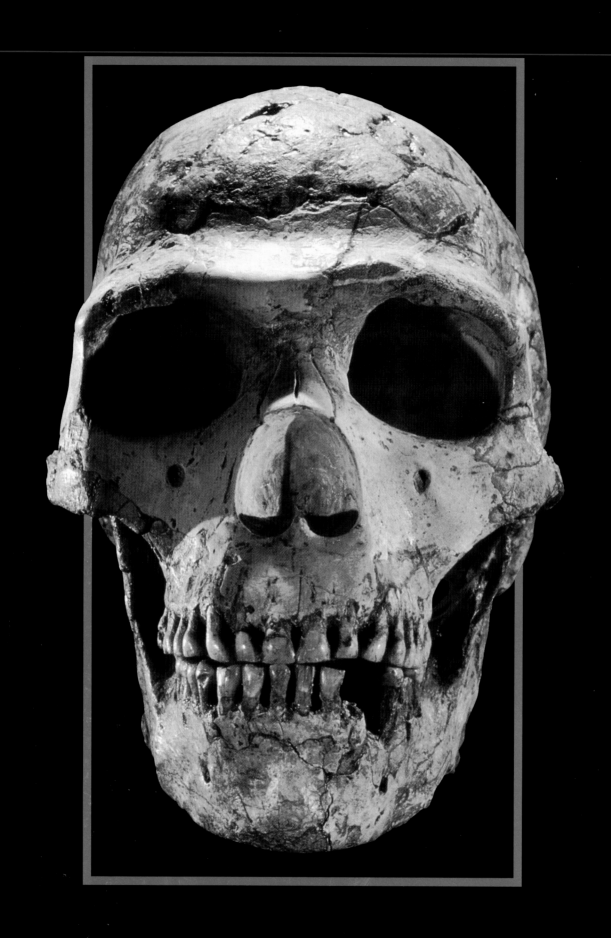

THE FIRST EUROPEANS: TRAVELERS ON AN EPIC JOURNEY

A frontal view of a Neanderthal skull shows the typical features of this early European: a heavy brow ridge, low forehead, and broad face. Neanderthals lived on the continent for over 100,000 years.

It was a sight to make a cave explorer's blood race; an opening large enough to enter, nine feet wide and three feet high, at the base of a cliff on the south coast of France just southeast of Marseilles. When Henri Cosquer noticed it in 1985, he had every reason to believe that no one had spotted it before. Looking closer, he saw that it was the mouth of a cramped but passable gallery that sloped gently upward into the rock. He had to find out where it led.

The difficulty was that the opening was deep under water, 110 feet beneath the surface of the Mediterranean Sea. Cosquer was a professional diver, with long experience in probing underwater grottoes, and he knew the risks of going in. Obviously, there was barely room between the gallery's roof and floor for a swimmer laden with air tanks to pass, and there was no way to know what lay ahead. If a swim fin struck the floor by accident, a centuries-long accumulation of fine silt would instantly cloud the water, making it impossible for the diver to see or to maintain orientation. (That the dangers were real would be confirmed six years later when three people who entered the gallery died there.)

After several surveys of the grotto's narrow entrance, Cosquer decided the risks were acceptable, and he returned to swim gingerly into the gallery that, as he was to find out, measured 450 feet long.

"It takes twelve minutes to get through," says archaeologist Jean Courtin, who made the swim later, "and believe me, those are twelve long minutes."

But the payoff was proportional to the danger. Just when it was beginning to feel like madness to continue, Cosquer popped to the water's surface. Peering into inky darkness illuminated only by his lamp, he saw that he was in an eerie, dank grotto some 180 feet long. Nearly half of it was submerged, the open areas spiked with large, ancient stalagmites and stalactites. Cosquer had taken the ultimate spelunker's risk and won the ultimate prize, becoming the first person to lay eyes on an underground world that had been sealed from human view for millennia. It was exciting enough, and he did not yet know the half of it.

Cosquer returned to the cave three more times in the next few years, but it was not until a dive in July 1991 that he noticed on a section of cave wall the stenciled outline of a human hand. Intrigued, he inspected the walls more closely. He found additional handprints, a variety of cryptic scratchings—then dozens of the scratchings and, most exciting of all, paintings depicting beasts not seen in Europe since the Ice Age. Henri Cosquer had discovered not just a cave, but a virtual museum of ancient art *(pages 10-13)*.

Subsequent research would show how the artists had gained access to the now-flooded chamber. On the portion of floor jutting from the water were the remnants of two fire pits, probably used for light, and a litter of charcoal, apparently from torches the artists had carried to illuminate their work. Radiocarbon dating indicated the charcoal was at least 18,000 years old; one piece dated to 27,000 years ago. That was a time of maximum glaciation during the last Ice Age *(page 15)*, when such an enormous amount of the world's water was frozen into glaciers that the Mediterranean was 360 feet lower than it is today, leaving its shoreline approximately seven miles away from the cave entrance.

Archaeologists have concluded that there were two periods of artistic activity in the cave—which they named Grotte Cosquer in honor of its intrepid discoverer. During the initial period, 27,000 years ago, a group of early modern humans, popularly called Cro-Magnons after the French cave in which their remains first were discovered in 1868, indulged in what appears to have been among humanity's earliest artistic impulses—stencils and tracings of hands. The drawings were random, simple outlines, some inscribed with fingers in the then-soft walls of the limestone cave. Grotte Cosquer was apparently abandoned for 8,000 years after these were done. Then, about 18,000 years ago, the cave was taken over by the Cro-Magnon animal artists.

As preserved on the walls of such magnificent underground galleries as Grotte Cosquer and Lascaux in France and Spain's Altamira, this cave art offers intriguing clues to the character of early humans. Apparently, according to Jean Clottes, president of the International Committee of Rock Art, early humans were "as sophisticated as we are, with religious feelings and an artistic sense." But the clues are scant and answers uncertain to the myriad questions raised by these ancient people whose descendants would later build Stonehenge and other great monuments throughout Europe; who would learn to use copper, and later bronze—the metal that would give its name to an epoch of human history stretching roughly from 2000 to 800 BC—and who would, in time, become the builders of modern European civilization.

Who were the cave artists, and how did they come to be in Europe, so far from humanity's ancestral home in Africa? And what was their relationship to the Neanderthals? Did they cause these people, dominant on the continent for 100 millennia, to disappear?

For years, a gravel pit near Boxgrove, England, on the coast of the English Channel southwest of London, had provided a bonanza for archaeologists and paleontologists. Working their way carefully down through the layers of sediment, they had unearthed abundant fossils of long-extinct elephants, rhinoceroses, bears, and tiny voles. And while they had seen plenty of indirect evidence that people had occupied the site—such as stone tools and flint chips—they had found no human remains.

Then, in late 1993, a team led by Mark B. Roberts, an archaeologist at University College, London, uncovered a fragment of a human skeleton. Although it was a small piece of evidence—an incomplete shinbone—it led to enormous conclusions. Roberts and his team identified the bone as the left tibia of a man, and calculated from its dimensions that he had stood about six feet tall and had weighed 180 pounds. "A robust male," said Geoffrey Wainwright, the chief government archaeologist for the group that financed the dig, "a man we would recognize as man today."

A LONG-FORGOTTEN ART GALLERY

When, in 1985, French diver Henri Cosquer found a partially water-filled cave in the south of France that had been isolated since the end of the last Ice Age, he had no idea of the treasure it held. But on a subsequent swim in 1991, he looked up to behold paintings and rock engravings. As temperatures increased and the ice sheets melted about 10,000 years ago, the Mediterranean rose to seal the grotto off from oxidizing and polluting air currents. The chamber's microclimate was preserved and so was its prehistoric artwork.

Using paints obtained by mixing charcoal with animal fat, Cro-Magnon artists lavishly adorned Grotte Cosquer, as the cave is known. Well over 50 handprints have been found there *(opposite)*, many now covered naturally with a protective layer of calcite. Many of the prints seem to be missing joints. Some scholars see the images as a kind of sign language, rendered by folding the fingers, which might have been used to identify individual species or perhaps to express some abstract idea.

Also covering the cavern walls are the images of more than 125 animals. While most of the beasts depicted—horses, bison, ibex, chamois, deer, and a large feline—can be seen in other French and Spanish Ice Age caves, only Grotte Cosquer includes such marine animals as auks, seals, and jellyfish.

No bones, flint flakes, or other indicators of daily life have been found in the cave, suggesting that this was a place where people spent little time. They may have used it as a kind of sanctuary, retreating there to perform rites involving the art.

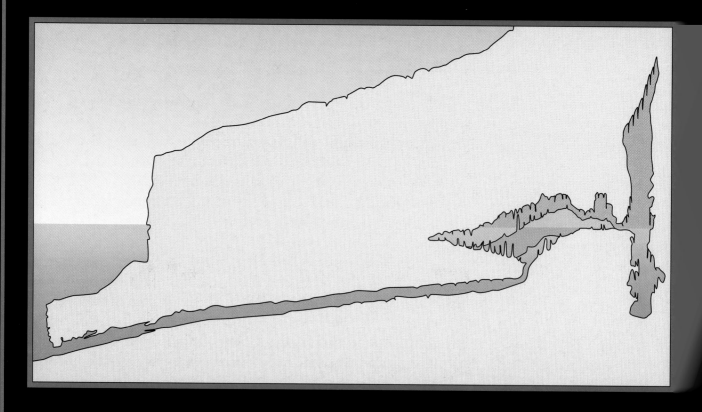

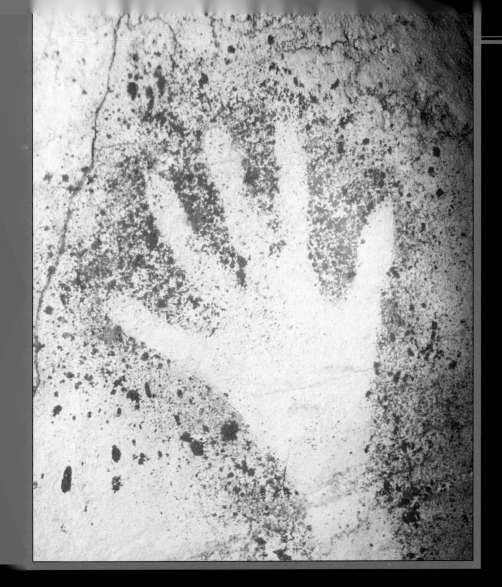

Stretched out as if in greeting, this disembodied hand is the first prehistoric artwork that Henri Cosquer saw when he reentered the cave in July 1991. The stenciled print was created by pressing a palm against the moistened cave wall, then blowing clay or charcoal dust through a hollow bone or with the mouth around the hand.

Beneath a stalactite-encrusted ceiling, Cosquer emerges from the water (below) during a visit to the cave in 1991. Although there was some discussion of making access easier by sinking a shaft down into the grotto, the idea was abandoned to protect the ancient art, which is at least 15,000 years older than that of the famed Lascaux Cave.

From an entrance at the base of a limestone shelf—over 100 feet beneath the Mediterranean—a narrow tunnel slopes for some 450 feet before opening into the huge chamber of Grotte Cosquer. As shown in this cross section, only half of the cave is above water, and it is in this air pocket that the wall paintings were found. Before rising sea levels flooded this subterranean network, Cro-Magnon visitors entered the cave on foot; today, a barrier across the entrance deters would-be intruders.

*Salt water laps at the bellies of two of three charcoal-
and manganese-painted horses that trot across one of
the walls of Grotte Cosquer. Many animals, long
covered by the rising water, have been obliterated; of
those that remain, one third are horses.*

*This sophisticated (to the modern eye) painting of a
black bison combines a three-quarter profile of the beast's
head and a side view of its body. Cro-Magnon artists
made use of this rare and realistic turned-head perspec-
tive to depict several animals in the cave.*

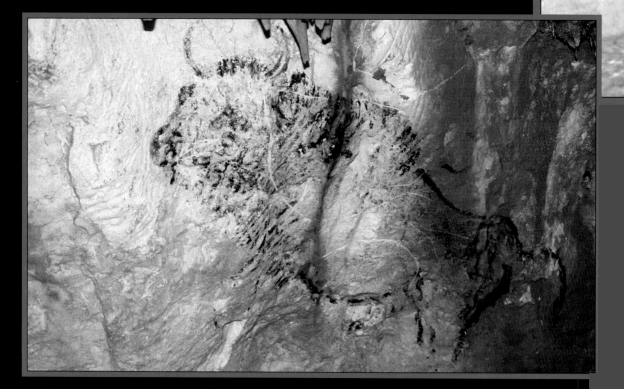

The stubby wings and portly shape of this penguinlike bird identify it as a great auk, a flightless seabird that became extinct about 150 years ago. The three auks that are represented in Grotte Cosquer are the only known examples of these birds in Paleolithic art.

What raised the status of the find from interesting to truly remarkable was a clue to its age found not in the bone—which was too old to be radiocarbon dated—but in the bone's immediate surroundings. Among the animal remains discovered nearby were jawbones of water voles whose molars displayed roots. It had already been conclusively established that water vole molars have not had roots for the past 500,000 years. Therefore "Roger," as the Boxgrove fossil came to be known to the scientists, had lived at least 500,000 years ago and was, in Wainwright's words, "our earliest European." One other human bone fragment, a jawbone unearthed in 1907 at Mauer, near Heidelberg, Germany, could be as old, but lacks Roger's conclusive dating.

Moreover, the Boxgrove man's fossil was found amid the evidence of his work, near the banks of an ancient stream where he had made flint tools and used them to butcher animal carcasses. The unprecedented association of the human remains and artifacts provided what Roberts described as the first solid information about the early stone toolmakers of Europe.

But for all it revealed about the earliest Europeans, the discovery still left shrouded in mystery the nature of their origins and makeup. They lived in the age of *Homo erectus,* who emerged from earlier human stock some two million years ago in Africa, several million years after the first hominids had branched off from the line that would also lead to modern chimpanzees. It is well established that some *Homo erectus* groups spread out of Africa into the Middle East and Asia more than one million years ago, but there are few clues as to when, or indeed whether, the species moved into Europe. Since the shinbone of the Boxgrove man could not offer conclusive evidence that it had belonged to a *Homo erectus,* some scientists tentatively grouped it in the separate, descendant species in which the Heidelberg fossil had earlier been placed—*Homo heidelbergensis*—at least until its place in evolution could be determined.

Scientists have found one thing common to all the stages of human development, from the earliest hominids of the African grasslands two million years ago to the socially and technologically advanced people who, by 10,000 to 12,000 years ago, had settled much of the Old World and moved into the New. During this immense span of time, all humans made use of tools fashioned from stone. Just as later stages of development would be named for the pottery humans created or the metal they worked, this longest era of human

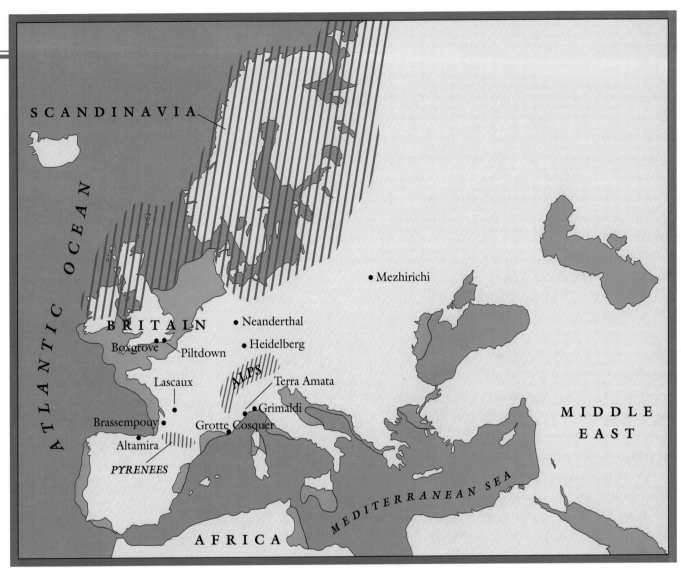

The schematic map above shows Europe at the time of the last glaciation, around 18,000 years ago. An ice sheet (blue shading) reaches down from the north into the British Isles, Scandinavia, and Russia, while smaller ones spread out from the Alps and the Pyrenees. Deprived of the water frozen in these vast sheets of ice—in places over 10,000 feet thick—the seas were lowered to reveal land that had previously been under water (red). Identified on the map are caves and other sites associated with major archaeological finds.

prehistory is known for the raw material of its technology—as the Paleolithic, or Old Stone Age.

That all these people should be known for their tools is inevitable, since the overwhelming majority of the evidence of their behavior during this nearly two-million-year span consists of the implements they used and discarded while camping, hunting, and butchering. Unlike flesh and bone or wood, stone does not decay, and hundreds of thousands of primitive tools have been recovered from where they were dropped tens and hundreds of thousands of years ago. For all their numbers, however, they provide a slender foundation for the many scenarios that have been built upon them, since no one can be absolutely certain about all the purposes they served or, for that matter, whether some of them were modified centuries—if not millennia—after their creation through human or natural intervention.

By early in the 20th century, the vast accumulation of stone artifacts had been placed into three broad categories. One type consists of hand axes that were formed by chipping a stone to fit it to the hand and sharpen its edge. These are the first surviving human tools, and the period during which they were used is known as the Lower Paleolithic. Eventually, hand axes were augmented by a greater variety of more-refined flake tools such as scrapers, usually made from flint nodules, whose preponderance defines the Middle Paleolithic. And finally, the Upper Paleolithic was characterized by the production of long thin flint blades, scrapers, and knives, and it also witnessed the beginnings of art—engraved objects and adornments of bone and ivory, and representational paintings on the walls of caves.

Across most of the Old World, the transition from Lower to Middle Paleolithic took place around 200,000 years ago, and the transition to the Upper Paleolithic 40,000 years ago. As might be expected from the fact that he lived some 500,000 years ago, the Boxgrove man was found surrounded by implements typical of the Lower Paleolithic.

But clear evidence of his stage of toolmaking reveals nothing about his biological species. Stone Age humans underwent two biological transitions whose timing corresponds very roughly to the changes in the nature of their tools. *Homo erectus*, who presided over 75 percent of the duration of the Stone Age in Africa, evolved in Europe and the Near East, at about the advent of the Middle Paleolithic, into *Homo sapiens neanderthalensis*, the first "wise" human—who was in turn succeeded as the Upper Paleolithic began by the subspecies *Homo sapiens sapiens*, referred to as the Cro-Magnons in Europe.

Boxgrove and Heidelberg fit neatly into this broad picture as *Homo erectus*. Given sufficient skeletal evidence to permit confirmation, however, another intriguing question would follow: Why did it take *Homo erectus* one million years to migrate into Europe from

Each working on a one-square-meter (10.8-square-foot) area marked by string and stakes, archaeologists sitting or lying on elevated planks excavate the 300,000-year-old site of Terra Amata, in Nice. Found during the 1966 dig were the remains of 21 oval beach shelters, each made of a framework of saplings buttressed by a ring of stones and held up by two or more stout posts, as depicted in the drawing at right. About 20 feet by 40 feet, they probably accommodated at least 20 people and are the oldest human dwellings in Europe.

Ubeidiya in Israel, or to move into the present-day republic of Georgia in the Caucasus, where they have been detected at a site 14 million years old, or even into Morocco, where fossil evidence places them one million years ago.

Only indirect evidence can lead closer to an understanding of who these early Europeans were, where they came from, and what role they played in the human habitation of the continent. The clues are to be found in what is known about the climate of the time and about the behavior of the continent's first inhabitants—who were, if not the Boxgrove man's immediate family, his close relatives.

The people called *Homo erectus* differed from their immediate predecessors primarily in size. They were much larger than their progenitors, boasting taller, heavier bodies. And starting about one million years ago, they evolved much larger brains. Their skulls were massive, broadest just above the ears, with a ridge called a nuchal torus at the back. Their large faces featured broad cheekbones and a bony ridge protruding at the line of their eyebrows. Their teeth, on the other hand, were smaller than those of their predecessors, apparently reflecting the fact that they made more use of tools than of their teeth in their daily tasks.

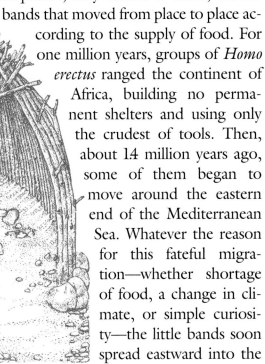

They lived off the land without benefit of any domesticated animals or plants. As a consequence, they existed in small, mobile bands that moved from place to place according to the supply of food. For one million years, groups of *Homo erectus* ranged the continent of Africa, building no permanent shelters and using only the crudest of tools. Then, about 14 million years ago, some of them began to move around the eastern end of the Mediterranean Sea. Whatever the reason for this fateful migration—whether shortage of food, a change in climate, or simple curiosity—the little bands soon spread eastward into the

Middle East, then northward into Asia Minor, eastward across southern Asia, and eventually westward toward Europe.

The implications of this change of venue were profound. Northward movement took humanity from the Eden of tropical Africa into the less salubrious environment of temperate Asia and Europe. On the average, the climate of southern Europe during the Ice Age was not unlike today's, but the slowly moving ice sheets that frequently crept southward over Britain and Scandinavia—as well as outward from the Alps and the Pyrenees—kept enormous expanses of the European continent locked for centuries at a time in uninhabitable, arid tundra. In the south, winters were long, cold, and cloudy.

These climatic conditions posed daunting problems for humans who had always depended on the ready accessibility of game and edible plants. Here, growing seasons were short, leaving food plants unavailable for large parts of the year. Animal populations were more separated and mobile. Survival would have required any number of things the primitive humans did not possess prior to 500,000 years ago: fire, shelter, and heavy clothing for warmth; the ability to harvest and store crops and to organize long-distance hunts. Initially, the migrating groups of *Homo erectus* faced this harsh new world, so different from the African homeland, with the advantages only of primitive tools and perhaps a few animal skins to augment their considerable body mass in protecting them from the cold.

All this has to be inferred from remarkably scant evidence of human habitation in Europe prior to 500,000 years ago. It consists primarily of pebbles whose shape frequently can be as easily ascribed to natural weathering as to human artifice. A few choppers and flakes, possibly of human manufacture, have been dated as 700,000 to 900,000 years old, in France, Italy, and Czechoslovakia. But no hand

THE HOAX THAT FOOLED THE WORLD

Excitement ran high at the Geological Society of Great Britain when it was presented with a fossil skull and apelike jaw in 1912. Here, at last, was the "missing link"—*Homo sapiens*'s supposed part-human, part-ape ancestor. To anthropologist Sir Arthur Keith and other members of the British scientific establishment envious of French and German prehistoric discoveries, it was a welcome find.

The bones had been unearthed at a gravel pit at Piltdown, Sussex, by amateur archaeologist Charles Dawson, assisted by the British Museum's Sir Arthur Smith Woodward *(seated, with Dawson, at left)* and French anthropologist and priest, Pierre Teilhard de Chardin. Still to come was the greatest discovery of all—that Piltdown man was a hoax.

Although there had been doubters from the start, only in 1949 did fluorine and other dating techniques raise serious questions about the real age of the fossils. Microscopic examinations revealed that a canine tooth from the site *(inset)* had been shaved to fit the jaw. Further study showed that the skull came from a modern human, and the jaw from an orangutan; the bones had been stained to match.

No one knows for sure who perpetrated the forgery. Most experts agree on Dawson's guilt but doubt he had the technical expertise to do it alone. While Woodward, the most obvious accomplice, is considered an innocent dupe, suspicion has fallen on at least 20 others—from Teilhard de Chardin, perhaps playing a Frenchman's prank on a country that had uncovered no human fossils, to writer Sir Arthur Conan Doyle, who lived nearby, knew Dawson, and was a member of the Sussex Archaeological Society. Most recently, however, the finger has been pointed at Keith. His motives: a driving ambition for academic advancement—and the establishment of an Englishman as the earliest European.

axes or cleavers—common in Africa for the previous million years—or human fossils have been positively shown to be older than the Boxgrove man.

Furthermore, the human fossils that begin to appear in the archaeological record with increasing frequency after the age of the Boxgrove fossil show puzzling differences from contemporaneous Asian and African remains. Scientists believe that these differences began to arise about 300,000 years ago as a result of long-term isolation of scattered groups of European early humans from their counterparts in Africa and eastern Asia. Some of these groups may have been wiped out; others, because of some evolutionary adaptation, survived, passing on the new attributes to their descendants—who would in turn evolve into what has become one of the best known of all the early human groups.

In 1856, near Düsseldorf, Germany, a crew of quarrymen came upon some human bones in a limestone cave in the Neander Valley. The short, stocky specimen (as the Neander remains indicated and later discoveries would confirm) had been no more than 5½ feet tall, with a barrel chest and heavy muscles. Over a conspicuous ridge of bone above the eyes, the forehead swept back to a low cranium that had a rounded protrusion at the back of the skull.

Ideas of evolution and natural selection were not yet widely accepted in 1856—indeed, it would be three years before Charles Darwin published his seminal work, *On the Origin of Species by Means of Natural Selection*—and few of those who pondered the German bones made any connection between the creature and any ancient ancestor of theirs. While some scientists of the time saw the Neander Valley skeleton as that of an early human, many others proclaimed it to be that of a misshapen Prussian soldier, a casualty of the biblical Flood, or a deformed congenital idiot.

In the subsequent decades, such dismissive explanations were increasingly difficult to reconcile with the discovery throughout Europe of similar remains, associated with stone tools and the bones and teeth of ancient animals. Eventually, in 1913, the French paleontologist Pierre-Marcellin Boule surveyed the finds and proposed that the distinctive remains were those of an extinct species of human, for which he used the previously proposed name *Homo neanderthalensis,* or Neanderthal man, for the site of the initial discovery. Later, when anthropologists learned of the previous existence of *Homo erectus* and others on the evolutionary tree, they realized that Neanderthals were in fact much closer to modern humans than to the earlier ancestors. The Neanderthals were accordingly reclassified in the 1950s as *Homo sapiens,* the same species as present-day humans, with the suffix *neanderthalensis* now indicating a separate subspecies.

Whatever their origins, *Homo sapiens neanderthalensis* displayed a number of adaptations that fitted them for the harsh climate of Europe at the time and for the work required to survive in it. Limbs foreshortened below the knee and elbow, which 19th-century analysts disparaged as apelike, had the advantage of conserving body heat better than, for example, those of tropical populations of *Homo erectus.* The large nose and puffy cheeks implied by the structure of the skull might strike modern humans as ugly, but they were well adapted to warming and moistening cold dry air, thus protecting the lungs and brain. And the large brain (slightly larger than that of modern humans and much larger than any earlier predecessors) was also a product of their need to find solutions to the problems presented by a harsh and difficult life.

There is evidence that Neanderthal teeth were used for a great deal more than chewing. This is indicated by the size and prominence of the front teeth and jaw, which facilitated the use of the teeth as a sort of third hand. Moreover, Neanderthal teeth characteristically show signs of wear not consistent with mere eating. In addition, many front teeth not only were worn, but also were marked with a series of diagonal scratches. This indicates that when eating, Neanderthals habitually bit off more than they could chew, and chopped off the excess with a stone knife wielded in perilous proximity to lips and teeth. The scenario is supported by the fact that almost all of the marks run from upper right to lower left, consistent with a self-inflicted scratch made by a right-handed person. Brain-cast studies and upper-limb asymmetry indicate that in most Neanderthals, as in most present-day humans, the left brain was dominant, a sign of right-handedness.

The earliest Neanderthal remains in Europe appear to be about 150,000 years old. By 110,000 years ago, Neanderthals were the only hominids in Europe and would continue to reign over the continent for another 70,000 years. At the time they first appear in the

European fossil record, the climate was, as it is today, in a mild interglacial period when the ice sheets had retreated to their minimum size. For the ensuing 70,000 years, the glaciers advanced into Britain and northern continental Europe, then rapidly retreated as another interglacial took hold.

The timing and duration of these events has been accurately established in recent years with the knowledge that different types of oxygen isotopes were predominant in the world's oceans during warming and cooling trends, and that they were preserved in the fossils of marine life deposited in ocean-floor sediments. This evidence led scholars to conclude that for about half the period Neanderthals lived in Europe, conditions were neither at their Ice Age worst or interglacial best, but in transition. The dominant feature of Neanderthal life over many millennia, then, was not bitter cold, but constant environmental change.

Even at the height of the Ice Age, the southern half of Europe supported an abundance of fish and game. The landscape was dominated by broad expanses of savanna—grassy plains across which drifted enormous and diverse herds of grazing animals and packs of

This reconstruction of a prehistoric hut discovered at Mezhirichi in the Ukraine is made of some 385 interlocking mammoth bones, including 95 reversed mandibles arranged in a herringbone pattern around the outside and a pair of tusks for an arched entrance; the bones were probably covered with animal hides and the chinks filled with moss, herbs, and grass. The huge bone house—16 feet in diameter and 23 tons in weight—dates from about 20,000 BC and was part of a settlement that contained four other such structures.

predators. A present-day counter-part does not exist, of course, but the closest comparison would be to the plains of Africa, not to some sparse subarctic region.

Although there is little solid evidence pointing to how the Neanderthals lived, much can be supposed from indirect knowledge—of the climate, the fauna, and the flora—and from historical knowledge of human and animal behavior. Numerous fossil animal bones found at living sites show that Neanderthal hunters were able to pursue and kill with stones and spears a variety of game—primarily reindeer, wild goats, and deer—but they also scavenged from the kills of large carnivores. This diet of meat would have been supplemented by nuts, berries, and other plant foods.

Neanderthals first sought shelter in the mouths of caves, but by 60,000 years ago they were also living in organized camps, building and maintaining well-established hearths, and moving across large territories with at least some purpose in mind.

Scientists have been able to study the fossil bones of Neanderthals of a greater span of ages than they have for previous hominid species. That the remains of children of earlier species are seldom found may simply be because they are relatively small, hence soon obliterated by natural processes. But the numerous remains of elderly Neanderthals suggests that on the whole they lived longer than did their predecessors—into their mid-forties, in some cases, with the average life expectancy appearing to have been about 30 years.

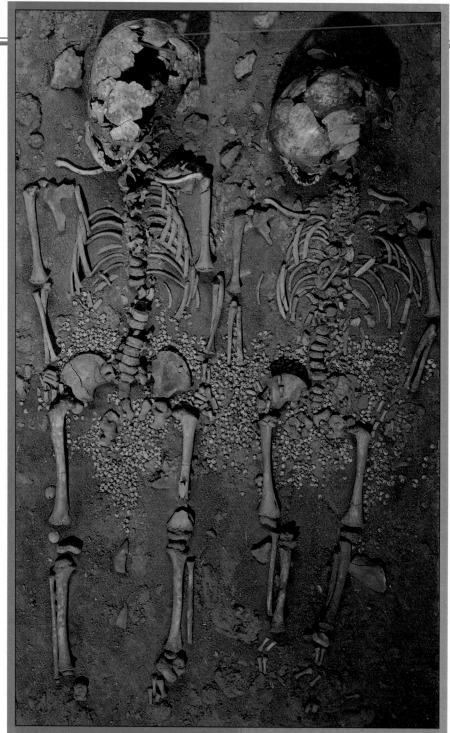

And the survival of more aged Neanderthals has another, more profound human implication. The very young and the very old require the care of others in order to survive. The nurturing of children can be ascribed to a biological imperative to perpetuate the species. But Neanderthals also appear to have cared as well for the aged and the infirm, preparing food for those who could no longer hunt or chew.

In addition to tending to the young and the old, Neanderthals apparently extended their caring to the dead. There is evidence of intentional burials in the caves of southwest Europe beginning about 100,000 years ago. In contrast to the scattered bits of bone that characterize the human remains of the preceding millennia, these bodies had been laid in specially dug pits, many of them further protected with an overlay of large rocks. Some scholars have interpreted adjacent finds of stone tools, bones, and pollen as evidence that Neanderthals put tools and supplies in the grave with the body, and laid flowers atop it.

If so, this could indicate a profoundly significant change in human behavior. The evidence of stone-tool cut marks on some human bones, as well as signs of marrow extraction, led several anthropologists to speculate that Neanderthals were cannibals. A change from eating bodies to ceremoniously interring them suggests far more than an aesthetically pleasing change of habits; it implies comprehension of abstract thoughts about such things as social roles and people as individuals, and the symbolic expressions of emotions with flowers (to indicate grief and good wishes), and perhaps even language to convey such ideas.

Despite their impressive biological adaptations to the environment, despite their advancing technological competence and increasingly sophisticated social organization, something happened to Neanderthals about 40,000 years ago. The fossil record shows that within the relatively short period of 10,000 years they were utterly replaced by the first modern humans, *Homo sapiens sapiens,* whose European branch is often referred to as the Cro-Magnons.

Here, as elsewhere, mysteries abound. Did Neanderthals become Cro-Magnons through evolutionary continuity? If so, what caused the sudden transformation, and how could it have occurred so quickly? If, on the other hand, Neanderthals succumbed to

Cro-Magnons, why did the adaptations that had carried Neanderthals successfully through 100,000 years of the Ice Age suddenly fail them, especially during a new period of relative climatic stability?

The most obvious distinction between Neanderthals and Cro-Magnons was anatomical. To begin with, the Cro-Magnon's skull had a completely different profile, lacking the Neanderthal's prominent ridge of bone over the eyes and the broad protrusion at the lower back of the skull. The Cro-Magnon's face was radically different from that of its predecessor, with smaller and less prominent front teeth and jaws, along with the forehead and chin that the Neanderthal lacked. The Cro-Magnon's frame was taller, more slender than the Neanderthal's, and the Cro-Magnon lived longer, more frequently into his fifties.

Technologically, as well as anatomically, Cro-Magnon and Neanderthal were worlds apart. Where Neanderthals had contented themselves with relatively heavy, crude implements, Cro-Magnons evolved finely worked, bladelike tools, some of them as elegantly thin and sharp as modern steel knives. Moreover, Cro-Magnons were not content, as Neanderthals had been, to replicate a few kinds of tools over and over for hundreds of generations. Cro-Magnons were innovators, and they rapidly developed more than 100 types of scrapers, chisels, and perforators, made of such things as bone and antler as well as stone. Nor were all the changes merely utilitarian; Cro-Magnons were developing an ever-stronger sense of design, of how things should look. Where tools had remained much the same for 100,000 years, rapid change now became the rule.

Just prior to 40,000 years ago, there were no humans in Europe who were not Neanderthals; after 30,000 years ago, there were no Neanderthals in Europe. Explanations for this are of three general types; one sees Neanderthal evolving into Cro-Magnon, another sees the Neanderthal completely replaced by Cro-Magnon. The third—and currently most common—explanation has it that early modern humans came into Europe from the Middle East and interbred with Neanderthals.

The number and accuracy of recent discoveries hazes over distinctions that once seemed clear. For example, a Neanderthal skeleton recently discovered in western France has been dated with a high degree of certainty to about 35,000 years ago. It is very difficult to

Forelegs tucked up against its belly and hindquarters fully extended, a carved horse appears to leap from the end of an 11-inch-long spear-thrower made from reindeer antler. Developed late in the Ice Age, this hunting tool acted as a lever for the end of a spear shaft and markedly increased the weapon's accuracy and range.

argue that one type of human could completely evolve to another in only 5,000 years.

More problematic for the continuous-evolution theory was the discovery in Israel of Cro-Magnon and Neanderthal remains in separate, but adjacent, caves. The fossils were too old for successful radiocarbon dating, but in 1988 a research team used a different technique on flints that had been burned in the fires of the different caves. When reheated, these emitted an amount of light proportional to the number of electrons that had been slowly and steadily trapped within them from the day they fell into the ancient fire. The technique, called thermoluminescence, yielded surprising results. The flints were more than 90,000 years old. It seems obvious that if Cro-Magnons were living in the Middle East 50,000 years before they appeared in Europe, those early modern humans could not have descended solely from Neanderthals.

Another source of speculation about the Neanderthal–Cro-Magnon sequence was opened up by advances in the field of molecular biology. Studies of DNA molecules—the microscopic building blocks of heredity—revealed that they are subject over very long periods of time to a constant rate of mutation of a kind that, while detectable, has no effect on the organism. The number of such neutral mutations present in any two individuals, then, would indicate approximately how long it has been since the individuals shared a common ancestor. In the late 1960s, biochemist Vincent Sarich of the University of California compared the DNA of apes with that of modern humans and calculated that the common ancestor of chimpanzees and humans lived between five million and seven million years ago. Previously, it had been assumed that the separation of the two species had occurred much earlier than that.

The results were even clearer when researchers used a DNA molecule from the mitochondria, the part of the human cell that provides energy. These molecules, referred to as mtDNA, are inherited only from the mother and accumulate neutral mutations fairly quickly, allowing scientists to establish their average rate of change and thus to track fairly precisely the evolution of the maternal line of ancestry.

In 1987, Allan Wilson, a biochemist at the University of California at Berkeley, analyzed the mtDNA of 147 individuals of various

Made by smoothing tiny slivers of bone, needles like the ones above provide clues to the survival of humans during harsh European winters. Using fine sinews as thread, they stitched skins and furs together to make tents and clothes.

This bone harpoon head is barbed on two sides and decorated with indentations that may be grooves for poison. In use by about 9000 BC, harpoons hafted to wooden shafts remained in place after piercing the hide of a prey animal, causing greater bleeding and a quicker death.

This 25,000-year-old flute made of bird bone points to the use of music by early Europeans. Flutes made from bird, bear, and reindeer bones have been discovered at the oldest of Upper Paleolithic sites.

races from around the world and came to the conclusion that they, and by inference all humans alive at the end of the 20th century, were descended from a woman who lived in Africa about 200,000 years ago. Although this hypothetical mother was immediately dubbed Eve, the calculation implied not that she was the only woman alive at the time, as in the biblical story of Eden, but that she was the only one whose lineage has survived until modern times.

Another, more haunting implication of this research is that both *Homo erectus* and Neanderthals, for all their splendid struggle with the Ice Ages and their nearly one million years of stubborn survival in Europe, were evolutionary dead ends. There is a broad gulf between the popular picture of humanity marching steadily toward ever-higher evolutionary ground and the idea of an entire human subspecies dominating Europe and the Middle East for millennia, then becoming extinct.

Many scientists, however, have questioned the mtDNA evidence. Among them is Milford Wolpoff, a paleontologist at the University of Michigan, who has observed that "you cannot ignore the male role in heredity" and draw important conclusions from only the female lineage. There is, he agrees, no doubt that all humans share a common origin in Africa: "We're more closely related to chimpanzees than any two frogs you see are probably related to each other." But he insists that all modern humans evolved from *Homo erectus* in their respective continents of Africa, Asia, and Europe, each group developing in the process its distinctive appearance. He sees, for example, an echo of Neanderthal's adaptation to cold in the large nose—"a real honker," says Wolpoff—that characterizes many present-day European faces.

The serpentine series of dots that cover this reindeer-bone plaque from a rock shelter in southwestern France may represent more than decorative Ice Age doodlings. One scholar has speculated that the incised marks on the four-inch-long tablet record the monthly phases of the moon.

Yet evidence to the contrary—that Cro-Magnons did not descend solely from, but rather replaced or interbred with Neanderthals—continues to accumulate. The fact that some examples of the finer blade work of the western European Upper Paleolithic period have been found in the hands of Neanderthals has been used to argue for evolution toward Cro-Magnon. None of those examples are more than 35,000 years old, however, and by that time Cro-Magnons, employing the new technology, were already well established in central Europe. Thus, it becomes even more likely that Neanderthals copied the advance than that they initiated it. Furthermore, the evidence strongly indicates that the technological advances spread at the same rapid rate, and throughout the same area, at the same time as the spread of the Cro-Magnons.

Thus it appears clear *Homo sapiens sapiens* lived in the Middle East at least 80,000 years ago, and then about 40,000 years ago spread into Europe. It is not necessary to assume that warfare, or even direct competition, was the cause of the rapid disappearance of Neanderthals. Computer models indicate that even a slight difference in the ratio of birth rates to death rates between the two groups—one that could be accomplished by a slight change in the availability of resources—could have resulted in the complete replacement of one population by the other within about 1,000 years.

While the end of the story—that Cro-Magnon continued while Neanderthal did not—is known and scientists are closer to knowing when and where their competition began, it is still unclear why events proceeded as they did. If the Neanderthals' swollen faces, stocky frames, and foreshortened limbs uniquely fitted them for their harsh Ice Age climate, why then were they supplanted by humans possessing none of these adaptations? And if the climate was the driving force behind the development of the limited Neander-

Stretching back to lick its flank, this bison once adorned the end of a reindeer-antler spear-thrower. The animal's pose, artfully carved with a razor-sharp flint, was dictated by the shape of the portion of antler used by the artist. Other creatures depicted on spear-throwers include ibex, felines, mammoth, birds, and fish.

thal technology, what accounts for the dramatically increased inventiveness of Cro-Magnons, who lived in an environment similar to the one the Neanderthals had experienced in their long dominance of the continent.

Of the many hypotheses advanced, among them shortages of raw materials or local privations caused by some climatic or economic shift, one is at the same time simple and profound. It suggests that everything Cro-Magnon so suddenly achieved derived from the invention of language.

While any such scenario is difficult to confirm through direct archaeological evidence, the appearance of language is nearly impossible to detect. But as archaeologists so frequently remind one another, absence of evidence is not necessarily evidence of its absence. However circumstantial and inferential its underpinnings, the concept of language as catalyst provides an elegant organizing principle for understanding the sudden development of the hallmarks of the Cro-Magnons' superiority.

Until the Neanderthals, and perhaps including them, hominids found their niche in the world largely through biological adaptation, a long, slow process of trial and error in which those fitted by genetic accident for survival passed along their superior attributes to their descendants. From Cro-Magnon onward, however, modern humans began to adapt to changing conditions almost exclusively by quickly and continually changing their culture—the way they hunted and traveled, the things they ate, the tools and shelters they used, the manner and extent of their travel. Concluding that such change is necessary, implementing it, then preserving it by explaining it to contemporaries and teaching it to children, requires the ability to reason—and to communicate the fruits of reason. In short, it requires a complex language.

Indirect arguments for the Cro-Magnons' greater use of language can be found in their superior organization. Cro-Magnon campsites were typically larger and more specialized than those of the Neanderthal, with constructed shelters and storage areas, and specific spots set aside for specific uses, and there was also a logical consistency to their location. Unlike the Neanderthal sites, which apparently were scattered, Cro-Magnon camps seem to have been concentrated along the established migration routes of their preferred game animals.

And Cro-Magnons had much stronger preferences in hunt-

The upper part of this tooth-and-shell necklace from the Dordogne region of France contains Dentalium shells that originated almost 100 miles away on the Atlantic coast. Three of the four large teeth at the bottom are bear teeth, and the fourth, second from the right, is an incised lion's tooth. The big cat still roamed southern Europe at the time, 30,000 years ago.

28

ing than did Neanderthals. Whereas the remains in Neanderthal camps indicate that they frequently ate whatever they found, Cro-Magnon sites more often show a high degree of specialization. In southwestern France, for example, 90 to 99 percent of Cro-Magnon garbage consists of reindeer remains. Other areas show similar concentrations of the remains of bison, mammoth, or deer.

Organizing one's camp, selecting its site, and hunting specific animals, it is argued, require complex language with which to express what one remembers and intends, to communicate plans, and to elicit cooperation. The expectation that planning and organization would produce a better and more reliable supply of food is borne out by evidence that Cro-Magnon populations increased as much as 10 times faster than those of the Neanderthal.

And if, as seems to be true, larger groups of people require more social and technological organization—that is, specialization of tasks and responsibilities—then it is only likely that Cro-Magnons began to assign rank to those fitted for responsibility and tasks to those best able to perform them. Once again, the scant physical evidence fits comfortably within this hypothesis. When toolmaking becomes the province of full-time specialists instead of the necessary chore of every hunter, the expected result is exactly what is found at Cro-Magnon sites—more finely worked implements, in a wider variety of specialized uses, employing more materials, than had ever been the case before. Cro-Magnons made unprecedented use of spear points, tools with handles, ornately decorated spear-throwers, barbed harpoons *(pages 24-25)*, and judging from ambiguous cave drawings, perhaps even cords, ropes, and nets.

If a society bestows rank, it needs to signify to the group the standing of special individuals—and Cro-Magnons, unlike Neanderthals, created emblems for personal adornment. Their burial sites and camps abound with ivory pendants, bead, shell and animal-tooth necklaces and bracelets. Enigmatic batons found at many sites—short reindeer-antler staffs perforated at one end and embellished with carvings of animals and birds—may have served as emblems of rank.

As impressive as were their achievements in tool-production and adornment, Cro-Magnons did something else that speaks eloquently of their awakening spirituality, creativity, and intellect. They devoted a great deal of time and effort to the crafting of objects with no apparent utilitarian purpose, whose sole function must have been to express an abstract idea about the nature of life. They created what today is referred to as art.

In 1852, while exploring a cave near Vienne, on the Rhone River in southeastern France, a French notary and his architect friend stumbled upon a fragment of bone. A portion of a reindeer's foot bone, it measured slightly more than five inches long and 1½ inches high. Carefully etched on its flat surface, in exquisite and anatomically correct detail, were two red deer. The scholarly authorities of the time, not yet aware of their own prehistory, attributed the etching to early Celts. Nine years later, however, the French scholar Édouard Lartet, after comparing the etching with a handful of other, similar discoveries of the preceding 30 years, declared it to be the work of a Cro-Magnon artist.

His pronouncement was by no means universally accepted. The assumption that early humans had been savages who did nothing but hunt, eat, and reproduce did not allow for the creation of artifacts of transcendent beauty. Decorations on a hunting implement might have been accepted, but the crafting of images for their own sake imputed to primitive people an aesthetic sense that the civilized people of the 19th century were not prepared to grant them.

Nevertheless, it soon became clear that the first such objects to be found on earth were created by the earliest modern humans in Europe. More than 30,000 years old, they are etched on or carved from rock and depict animals and (in fewer cases) humans. By 15,000 years ago the so-called portable art form had spread with Cro-Magnons all across Europe, although with puzzling inconsistencies. Many sites yield no portable art at all, others have a smattering, while certain sites contain thousands of pieces—in eastern Spain one cave alone housed 5,000 engraved and painted plaques along with scores of decorated bones.

By that time, craftsmen were producing realistic statuettes of the animals they regularly killed for food—from mammoth and reindeer through fish and birds—in stone, ivory, antler, and even fired clay. They accompanied many of their works with complex arrangements of dots and lines whose meanings are lost, although several modern researchers see in some of them representations of lunar or climatic cycles that might have been propitious for hunting *(page 26)*. Well over 10,000 pieces of portable art have been identified.

SURPRISE IN AN ANTIQUES SHOP WINDOW

Canadian sculptor Pierre Bolduc could not have known it at the time, but the display of female figurines he admired in the window of a Montreal antiques shop in 1990 were some of the oldest pieces of art in the world. He bought the tiny carvings for around $10 each. It was not until three years later, when he showed them to anthropologist Michael Bisson *(right)*, that he discovered they were Venuses, dating back 18,000 to 25,000 years.

Dozens of similar prehistoric ivory and stone Venuses have turned up at sites all across

Europe. Most have in common huge breasts, thighs, and buttocks, with head, arms, and legs rendered in token fashion. Such exaggerated features seem to show the importance of procreation, which suggests that the figurines may have been used in a widespread fertility cult.

How had the Venuses come to Montreal? The story begins in 1883, when French amateur archaeologist Louis Julien found 15 tiny Stone Age carvings at Grimaldi near Monte Carlo. After selling seven to a Paris museum, including the one at left, Louis Julien immigrated to Canada in 1895, taking the remaining eight with him. Harvard's Peabody Museum managed to acquire one of the images in the 1940s, but the others disappeared from sight until they turned up in the antiques shop. Unaware of their great value, two elderly Julien descendants had sold them to the owner.

When Cro-Magnon artists turned their attention to the human form, they usually represented a female. Indeed, for a 2,000-year period beginning approximately 25,000 years ago, artisans all across Europe produced an abundant quantity of so-called Venus figurines, depictions of robust, well-fed women with large breasts and buttocks and attenuated heads and limbs. Because the Venuses proliferated at a time of unusual climatic change, when the weather was turning colder and cooperation among various groups might have been the key to survival, some researchers have seen these figures of plenty, of the good life, as a possible medium of exchange or even as prestigious gifts, presented by one leader to another to ensure continued good relations between them.

Two decades after the discovery in a French cave, the existence of Cro-Magnon portable art was well documented. Yet the scientists of the time remained utterly unprepared for a final, stunning revelation of the artistic abilities of Cro-Magnons, a discovery brought to their unwilling attention by an amateur.

Don Marcellino de Sautuola, a gentleman landowner of Cantabria on the north coast of Spain, was an intellectually curious man. In 1878, when he was 47, he traveled to the Paris Universal Exhibition, where he was transfixed by the displays of Paleolithic portable art. He visited them again and again, and discussed their collection and significance with France's preeminent prehistorian, Édouard Piette.

Inspired to begin his own collection of ancient figurines, Sautuola began scouring the floors of caves in the Cantabria region. Eventually, in November of 1879, his new passion drew him back to a cave in Altamira he had visited briefly three years before. He took his young daughter Maria with him into the cave, and while he probed the floor intently for buried treasure, she wandered idly around the cavern. While playing, she did something no other visitor to the cave had done since its discovery in 1868—she looked up. "Papa, Papa," she cried delightedly, "look—painted bulls!"

When Sautuola followed his daughter's gaze upward, he became the first person in modern times to comprehend the finest artistic achievement of his Cro-Magnon forebears. He was looking at a painted group of Stone Age bison, each more than five feet in length, their colors applied in what seemed to him to be a fatty paste. Some of the animals in the center of the group were curled up as if in death, others were standing and facing outward toward a group of human figures. Sautuola saw immediately the similarity in style to the animals of the statuettes he had been seeking, and intuitively knew what was confirmed only much later—that these paintings had been crafted 15,000 years before.

Unfortunately, Sautuola was a novice, not an established paleontologist. And he lived in Spain at a time when all the important Stone Age finds were in southwestern France. Moreover, the scientific establishment, which had only with great resistance accepted the fact that primitive people could carve, was not willing to admit that they could also paint. With only one exception, Sautuola's discovery was greeted not only with skepticism but with ridicule and accusations of fraud from eminent authorities who refused even to visit the cave and look at the pictures. In 1888, in despair that his find had been so roundly disdained, Sautuola died.

Not until 1902, after the discovery of several other cave paintings, each of them dismissed at the time as the work of children or con artists, did the scholarly community finally accept what had by then become unarguable: that Cro-Magnons had left in cave galleries throughout southwestern France and northern Spain a magnificent collection of paintings.

Almost all cave art represents animals, both prey (wild cattle, reindeer, horses, bison, red deer, mammoth) and predator (lions, bears, wolves). Only a few human forms appear, and unlike the realistic animals, they are often enigmatic, appearing to be half-human and half-animal, or in other respects having cryptic characteristics.

The works are found deep in caves, not near the entrances where people lived. Some are outlines etched in the stone walls with flint blades, others are paintings colored with the yellow-to-red tints of iron ocher and black manganese dioxide. The pictures are often associated with handprints, various geometrical forms, and arrange-

The low ceiling of Altamira's Painted Hall comes alive with two of the almost-lifesize bison seen by young Maria de Sautuola in 1879. More than pieces of art, such prehistoric cave paintings probably had ritual or ceremonial importance: Before the hunt men may have gathered in these caves and engaged in rituals contrived to increase their prowess by confronting the animals they had to stalk.

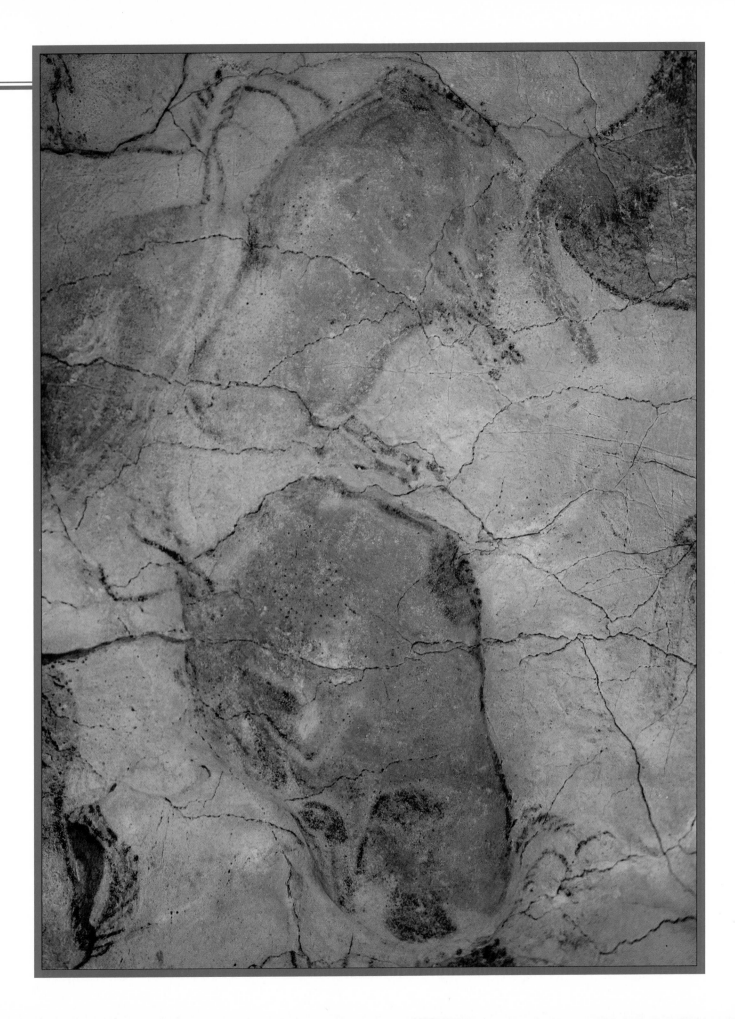

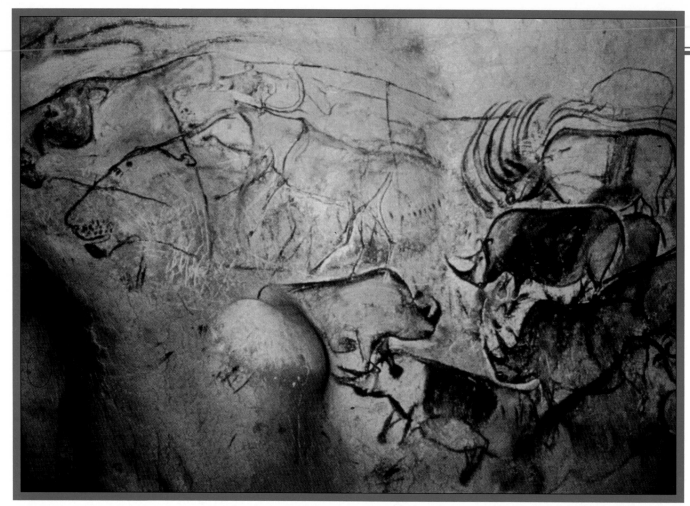

ments of dots and lines, some of which were placed over earlier paintings, almost obliterating them. This casual defacing of existing work suggests the pictures were neither done nor admired as art, but as symbols whose significance changed over time.

Perhaps the animals represented were the totems of certain communities, or perhaps the artist intended to gain some magical control over the animal by capturing and manipulating its image. Some see the paintings as depictions of hunts designed to convey information about hunting techniques. Others conclude that they were executed by shamans who were portraying their intermediary role between the needs of hunters and the spirits of animals. Perhaps they were used as part of seasonal rituals.

The increasing knowledge about cave art through the early decades of the 20th century was accompanied by surprise discoveries that revealed the volume and scope of these ancient works. In September of 1940, for example, four teenage boys scrambled into a deep hole on a hill near Montignac in southwestern France. Barely able to squeeze through the passageway, they came at last to a large cavern, near whose entrance they noticed a series of lines and spots in black

Drawn at least 20,000 years ago, wooly rhinos and big cats seem to move across the wall of a multichambered cave discovered near Avignon in southern France on December 18, 1994. Among the hundreds of animal depictions are the earliest known portrayals of a panther and an owl. Upon viewing the beautifully executed and perfectly preserved drawings for the first time, one French rock art specialist said, "I was so overcome that I cried. It was like going into the attic and finding a da Vinci."

and red on the walls. Then they entered a large chamber. In the light of their torches they saw an astonishing array of images—great bulls, unicorns, black horses, and red deer.

The news of the boys' discovery sparked an initial rush of interest, but World War II intervened. The cavern was virtually forgotten until 1948, when local entrepreneurs improved it, adding a grand entrance chamber with massive bronze doors, stairways for easy access to the cave, and electric lights for unimpeded viewing of the paintings. Then they opened the cave, now known as Lascaux, as a tourist attraction.

Crowds of visitors, averaging 600 per day, introduced so much moisture into the cave through respiration that condensation on the walls began to sprout mold on the paintings. After those problems were solved by the addition of a massive air-conditioning system in 1958, the numbers of visitors grew to 1,500 per day. Then, blotches of algae and bacteria began spreading across the ancient images. Finally, in 1963, the French government closed the cave to the public, restored its environment to the natural conditions that had preserved the wall paintings through the ages, and restricted access, allowing only infrequent visits by scientists and scholars.

Art of a different kind—an extensive gallery of 20,000-year-old animal images scratched into rocky outcroppings in northwest Portugal's Côa River gorge—came to light in late 1994, just four years before the entire gorge was slated to be inundated by the waters of a massive hydroelectric-dam project. And while archaeologists hope to preserve the site for future study, it is likely that cave images will remain the primary source of knowledge about the work of prehistoric artists.

As with portable art, cave art varies greatly in quantity from site to site. Of the 300 or so decorated caves found so far in Europe, most contain only a handful of images while a few, such as Lascaux and Altamira, contain hundreds or even thousands. And archaeologists continue to be tantalized by the realization that many subterranean galleries of ancient art still await discovery. Indeed, in January 1995 the French government revealed that a trio of investigators, exploring in a region southeast of Lascaux, had recently come upon a previously unknown complex of grottoes that may prove to be the most extensive trove of cave art yet found.

Intriguingly, only a very few caves boast an abundance of both portable and cave art. This suggests that portable art may have been created in the living area for daily use, while cave art was reserved for sanctuaries and special occasions.

No cave art has been found in central Europe, between northeastern France and the Urals, although plenty of portable art has been uncovered in that region. Cave art is concentrated in the southwestern river valleys of France and along the northwestern coast of Spain. This was the southernmost extent of the grassy plains of glaciated Europe and the probable route of the migrating herds of animals that flourished in such an environment.

About 10,000 years ago, however, all that began to change—rapidly by archaeological standards, perhaps imperceptibly to the Cro-Magnons, but implacably and fatefully. The great ice sheets receded to the north, and the oceans rose with the flood of meltwater, inundating coastal plains and land bridges, such as the one that existed as recently as 8,500 years ago between today's Great Britain and the European continent. Dense forests spread northward across central Europe, and the large migratory herds of grazing animals were driven before them, leaving behind only about one-quarter of the animals that once had flourished in the southern European steppe. Humans were faced with two hard choices—either follow their familiar food sources, or stay behind and adapt to dramatically changed conditions. Those who stayed, survived, but at a terrible price. Their numbers were drastically reduced, their settlements became smaller and more dispersed, their lives more difficult. They regressed to simpler, cruder tools, discarded much of their social structure and with it the associated adornments.

While the business of survival remained grim for both groups, these first true Europeans were about to take another great cultural leap, one that would soon lead to monumental achievements undreamed of by earlier toolmakers and cave artists.

THE MYSTERIOUS STONES

Among the most abiding mysteries of Europe are the great stone monuments, or megaliths. Why most were erected no one can say definitely. What is certain is that they are the first stone structures anywhere to have been put up on such a massive scale.

Some of the megaliths were apparently erected to align with the sun and the moon at critical junctures in the solar and lunar gyrations, perhaps as a method of tracking time and of predicting seasonal changes. Other monuments may have been used as ritual centers and as social gathering sites. And still others can be identified as tombs.

Megaliths break down into four categories: solitary standing stones, known as menhirs; groups of menhirs, such as stone circles; roofed chambers; and temples. Roofed chambers—numbering thousands in Europe—are the most common. Such tombs may be completely or partially buried under a mound of earth or rocks, or they may be freestanding. The purpose of single menhirs is more ambiguous; several have been found to have burial remains at their base, while others seem to represent astronomical markers of some kind. Le Grand Menhir Brisé in northwestern France, which now lies horizontal and broken, is believed to have once stood 67 feet tall. Raising it would have been an incredible engineering feat that involved the intellectual and muscular power of the local populace.

Menhirs are often grouped in rings or rows, though the rings occur only in Great Britain and Ireland. Stonehenge *(above)*, on England's Salisbury Plain, is perhaps the most famous of all the rings. Remodeled several times over the centuries, Stonehenge was planned around a symmetrical axis that points toward the direction of the summer sunrise.

Viewed here in the morning mist are a few of the more than 2,000 megaliths that stretch in 12 rows for nearly a mile near Carnac, in northwestern France. The function of this second-millennium-BC monument is uncertain. One theory holds that the stones constituted a huge lunar observatory made up of multiple megalithic sites, including two other alignments nearby.

Silhouetted by the rising sun, the 1800-BC stones at Callanish on the remote isle of Lewis with Harris in the Outer Hebrides of Scotland were once covered by a peat bog. From a small central ring of thin pillars, with a burial chamber at the foot of the tallest megalith, the stones extend along avenues to the four points of the compass. One avenue descends toward the waters of Loch Roag, making the site a possible source for the legend that megaliths go down to the water to drink.

The 13-foot-long capstone of the Poulnabrone Dolmen presents a stark profile in evening light on a deserted limestone plateau in southwestern Ireland. This type of roofed chamber, known as a portal dolmen, is most prevalent in Ireland, where there are more than 150 similar structures. Portal dolmens apparently served as tombs for honored dead or as entrances to more elaborate burial vaults.

SEARCH FOR PERMANENCE IN UNSURE TIMES

Thought to portray a masked deity revered by some of Europe's first farmers, this clay figure wields a symbol of power unknown to their hunter-gatherer predecessors: a sickle. Archaeologists discovered the 6,500-year-old sculpture in Hungary.

Nestled in the hilly border country of Wales, the quiet town of Welshpool seemed an unlikely spot for a major find reaching all the way back to Britain's prehistoric past. The few paltry ancient remains that existed in the area could hardly rival the concentrations of giant monuments 100 miles to the southeast, in the rolling plains of the English county of Wiltshire. Yet the site was to yield its own contribution to the continuing quest to decipher one of archaeology's most persistent mysteries: the origins of the great monument of Stonehenge.

In the winter of 1990-1991, highway construction near Welshpool prompted the local Clwyd-Powys Archaeological Trust to excavate Sarn-y-bryn-caled, a site perched on a terrace above the Severn River, two miles south of the town. Fifteen years earlier, aerial photographs of the terrace's crest had revealed the existence of a circle 65 feet across, marked by the subtle traces of 20 long-filled-in pits in a ring around a central pit, 15 feet in diameter.

Now the excavators discovered that the pits, distinguished by their in-filling of pink silty soil from the river gravel of the area, had been circular holes more than three feet deep. In their bottoms lay rotted fragments of the sturdy 12- to 15-inch-thick wooden posts that they had once held. The central pit, where six posts had stood so close together that their holes overlapped, contained what was left of

a cremated young adult, buried there around 2100 BC. Among the ashes lay four flint arrowheads, the apparent instruments of death. To the trained eyes of the archaeologists, the weapons seemed of too fine a standard of craftsmanship for the victim to have died in battle or as result of a hunting accident. Rather, he or she may have been killed as a sacrifice.

Sarn-y-bryn-caled was by no means the only such ring to come to light in Britain. Remains of a wood circle had been found as far back as 1925, not far from Stonehenge itself; evidence of other such structures followed. Between 1925 and 1991, British archaeologists debated whether these circles might mark the sites of wood buildings whose walls and roofs had decayed. In their efforts to reconstruct Sarn-y-bryn-caled in February 1991, the excavators first tried to rebuild it as a covered dwelling. But the 25-foot span between the outer and inner circles of 10-foot-high posts appeared too wide for the large timbers needed to support a roof; they reported that the uprights seemed "an unintelligible forest of posts."

The archaeologists then hit upon a novel, almost mischievous idea. It had long been known that the people who raised Stonehenge late in the third millennium BC were accomplished woodworkers. In fact, to build the monument—which was erected in three main stages

Gruesome but not fatal, the tip of an arrow remains lodged in the hard palate of a man killed 5,400 years ago, in the early Neolithic period. Archaeologists surmise that death came after a second arrow pierced his breastbone, most likely severing an artery. The angle of the arrow in the palate suggests that the archer may have been sitting in a tree. Skull and breastbone were found in a Danish grave.

over the course of 1,500 years—the ancient Britons had replicated their familiar carpentry techniques, using laboriously carved mortise-and-tenon and tongue-and-groove joints to keep the massive horizontal crosspieces, or lintels, in place on their uprights, even though the weight of the stones made them unnecessary. With this in mind, the reconstruction team proceeded to connect the tops of the outer posts with wooden lintels—and the unintelligible forest suddenly became a "woodhenge."

Carbon-14 dating of Sarn-y-bryn-caled and the other similar finds showed that the structures were contemporary with or earlier than Stonehenge. Now, the excavation and reconstruction of Sarn-y-bryn-caled suggested, Stonehenge might not just have been built by woodworkers, but may itself have been based on a wooden prototype. In a land yet heavily forested, timber would have been a readily available building material. Easier by far to work than stone, wood had one disadvantage: its impermanence.

Of all the stone circles of Britain, Stonehenge remains unique. Across the grasslands of southern England, ancient peoples laboriously hauled huge blocks of stone and, in a remarkable feat of engineering, erected them in precise circular arrangements of uprights and lintels that for almost four millennia have bewitched public and experts alike. Few structures have provoked so many interpretations. At various times, the suggested builders of Stonehenge have included the Druids, dwarfs, Irish giants, Merlin the magician, the Romans, extraterrestrials— and even the devil. The function of Stonehenge has inspired still more speculation: It has been called a temple, an ancient computer, a cemetery, a sacrificial altar, a cattle pen, a polling booth, a marker for spacecraft, and a switch box for the magnetic currents of the earth.

But Stonehenge is not the only conundrum. It is just one part of a prehistoric European landscape rich in ritual significance and archaeological mystery. All across the British Isles and the Continent, earthwork banks and ditches mark out enclosures and avenues; postholes testify to rotted timber structures, grassy mounds called barrows cover rock-built tombs, and immense stones raised at the cost of huge effort proclaim the determination of early Europeans to build for themselves enduring monuments. In lands stretching from the Mediterranean island of Malta to the remote Scottish Orkney Islands in the North Sea, thousands of stone constructions—called megaliths, or great stones—stand in rings, in lines, as solitary boulders, and in table-topped tombs and temples, striking memorials to the genius of a long-vanished people.

Such is the technical mastery evinced in handling these great stone blocks that archaeologists earlier this century assumed that the creation of the monuments lay beyond the abilities of the supposedly barbarian Europeans. The skills required, they argued, could only have been acquired from the great civilizations of the East. Noting the particular concentration of structures along the Atlantic coast, the archaeologist V. Gordon Childe early in the 20th century proposed that "megalithic missionaries" had traveled northward along the land's edge, spreading the techniques of stone construction to savages who had little or no knowledge of the material. Any regional differences between megaliths, Childe believed, could be explained by the practices of the local populations that adopted them. According to this so-called diffusion theory, the source of the tradition was obvious: The stone structures of Europe were clearly imitations, albeit crude ones, of the sophisticated stone-block buildings of the Mycenaeans, who dominated the Aegean around 1500 BC.

In the 1960s, however, the development of radiocarbon dating allowed scholars to calculate the age of organic material by measuring the rate at which its carbon atoms decay. For Stonehenge, the new technique dated bone, peat, charcoal, and other matter associated with the great stones—and effectively killed off the diffusion theory. It proved that megalith-building flourished from around the fifth to the third millennia BC, during the period known as the Neolithic, or New Stone Age. In other words, a good 2,000 years before the Mycenaean civilization arose.

For an understanding of the megaliths, archaeologists were forced to turn back to temperate Europe itself. Based on excavations, ethnographic studies of modern tribal peoples around the world, and painstaking reconstructions of prehistoric European life, they created a picture of a society that was more complex and sophisticated than had previously been imagined. They found that from around 7000 BC, when farming first appeared on the Continent, lifestyles based on planting crops and rearing livestock slowly spread across all of Europe. The change brought new ways of living: new settlements, new trade networks, new crafts and technologies, new social orders, new beliefs, and new monuments.

In the river valleys of the Balkan Peninsula, which now comprises Bulgaria and the states of the former Yugoslavia, large mounds called tells offer rich pickings for archaeologists inquiring into the lives of early Europeans. Accumulations of earth and debris, the tells testify to periods of human occupation over several millennia. At Karanovo in Bulgaria, for example, 2,000 years' worth of weathered earth from mud-daubed walls and everyday

waste created a mound that measures 270 yards by 160 yards.

Karanovo's lowest level, dating from the second half of the sixth millennium BC, yields some of the earliest evidence of an important development that was then taking place in Neolithic societies. Among the outlines of simple wood-framed huts arranged in parallel rows—making in total a village of perhaps 30 houses and between 100 and 150 inhabitants—excavators discovered sickles made from deer antlers with flint pieces stuck into them. Often the sickles were found beside the central cooking hearth, along with millstones, pottery bins for storing grain, and ovens for drying grain. Farming had arrived in Europe.

From the time that humans first lived on the Continent, they had survived by hunting and gathering. The people of the Mesolithic, or Middle Stone Age, that inhabited its rolling, almost unbroken woodlands followed nomadic lives, killing wild animals, catching fish, and gathering seeds, fruit, nuts, and berries. But now, around 7000 BC, they began to build more permanent settlements, carefully sited in the middle of fertile land that would support the new crops that helped spur the change. Archaeologists deduce from the analysis of ancient seeds winnowed from the detritus of ancient sites that wheat and barley, neither thought to be native to Europe, were introduced from the lands of the Middle East, as were the sheep, pigs, and goats that European farmers increasingly raised.

The Neolithic revolution, as scholars once styled these changes, was in fact nothing of the sort, if revolutions are thought of as being quickly over. Despite the profound developments that were

Neolithic farmers who lived on the shore of Chalain, a small mountain lake about 40 miles northwest of Geneva, Switzerland, used parts of deer antlers to make handles for the tools shown above: an ax (top) and an adz. Wielding such stone-bladed implements, European agriculturists cleared virgin land for cultivation.

A masterpiece of a dying craft, this 11½-inch flint dagger from the Danish island of Fyn mirrors the shape of cast-metal weapons that would soon make it obsolete. Although it is a testament to the skill achieved by flintsmiths at the end of the Stone Age, such a design was ill suited to the brittle stone, suggesting that this piece may have been knapped more for display than for practical use.

under way, modern investigation has highlighted the gradual, confused nature of the process. Archaeological finds at Starčevo, a tell near the Serbian capital, Belgrade, indicate that the early agriculturists—the term archaeologists use to describe these small-scale farmers—continued to supplement their diet by hunting. Bones at the site show that in addition to keeping their own domesticated animals, the inhabitants ate red and roe deer, wild cattle, horse, and boar; wild ducks, geese, and swans; and pike, catfish, bream, and carp. But just who these first farmers were remains unclear. Most probably, they were colonists from the East who migrated into Greece and the Balkan Peninsula, bringing with them their farming ways, their seed crops, and their animals. The new arrivals might have passed on their knowledge to the indigenous hunter-gatherers, some of whom may also have adopted the new, more sedentary lifestyle. At seminomadic settlements that already existed before farming began, deposits of bones indicate that after the coming of agriculture, the inhabitants' diet actually changed little: They still ate mainly what they could hunt from the land or fish from the rivers. It would take 3,000 years before agriculture would become the chief means of survival for Europeans.

Even for Neolithic communities, the scale of farming operations at this time was probably quite limited. Pollen studies show that the Europe of 9,000 years ago was far more heavily wooded than it is today, and it would have been difficult for the early agriculturists of the Balkans, armed only with stone axes, to clear large areas for cultivation. And if they did not practice crop rotation and the manuring of fields to reinvigorate the soil, yields would have gone down over the years until the area's soil was eventually exhausted. Archaeologists working in the Maritsa Valley of Bulgaria in the early 1970s

WHEELS THAT MADE EUROPE GO ROUND

The turn of humanity's first wheel was once ascribed to the ingenuity of Middle Easterners; now the origin of this revolutionary invention is a mystery, as archaeologists ponder examples of Europe's earliest wheels. The oldest wheel-related artifact, the Bronocice Vessel *(above, right)*, was discovered in Poland in 1974. Made about 3400 BC, it is some 200 years older than similar pictorial evidence previously found in Iraq. Incised in its clay are four-wheeled wagons interspersed with vertical designs suggesting trees, a zigzag line probably representing a river, and a checkerboard pattern that may depict active and fallow fields.

Europeans had already been farmers for 2,000 to 3,000 years when the wheel appeared. Attached to wooden wagons in single or double pairs, the wheel gave them a mode of transportation that not only enabled them to move about but also allowed them to collect crops for storage or carry them to market.

Europe's earliest wheel (right), *20 inches wide and dated to about 3200 BC, turned up in the chalky limestone soil at the bottom of Switzerland's Lake of Zurich. Its once-circular shape has been altered by decomposition and the pressure of the surrounding sediment.*

The shapes of the two wooden wheels above are shown as first seen by the Russian archaeologists who excavated them in 1987, near the Kuban River east of the Black Sea. The wheels came from one of many graves in an area in which wagons were buried about 2500 BC. Although the wood has long since decomposed, the remains, blended with the dirt, have hardened. The white substance was left by decayed reeds that once covered the burial.

Clay cups (right), in the form of four-wheeled carts, are the oldest models of wagons found in Europe. The cups were buried with their owner in a grave north of Budapest, Hungary, between 2700 and 2400 BC. Their high, sloping sides suggest that the carts they were modeled on were used to haul agricultural products. Other early representations of wagons, uncovered throughout Europe, demonstrate the wheel's rapid and wide-ranging spread.

came up with one possible explanation of how the Balkan farmers might have gotten around the problem of small yields. They suggest that settlements in the valley were carefully placed three miles apart to reduce overexploitation of the land and deliberately sited close to different types of fertile soil suitable for various crops. A comparison with primitive peoples who live in the same way today suggests that even without intensive farming, such an area could comfortably support 150 people.

The success of the agriculturists is evident from the height of the tells themselves. The mound at Vinča, near Starčevo, for example, stands 30 feet high and gave its name to a great culture that arose in the Balkans around 5000 BC and survived for three millennia. Vinča is in some ways little different from earlier settlements, in that people still lived in oblong houses made of wattle and daub—straw, soil, and other materials applied over woven branches—whose gabled roofs are indicated by a central row of postholes where supporting timbers would have been placed. But it also provides evidence of the relative sophistication that came with a sedentary life and permitted the development of craft activities: Excavators have found a fine, black, burnished pottery that replaced the earlier plain ware and have uncovered traces of an increasingly sophisticated system of trade and exchange. Like other Balkan tells, Vinča yielded beads and bracelets made from a seashell of the *Spondylus,* a mollusk found in the Aegean Sea, 250 miles to the southeast. And obsidian—a glasslike volcanic mineral used for cutting tools—may have come from islands in the Mediterranean. Whether through the transportation of goods over long distances or through a series of exchanges from one settlement to another, the horizons of the Europeans were broadening.

From its earliest cultures, the Neolithic way of life—with the quest for farmland as its driving force—spread out to cover much of the Continent. Based on the appearance of distinctive styles of pottery, archaeologists have traced the movement of agricultural colonists in two main directions during the sixth and fifth millennia BC. Westward along the shores of the Mediterranean Sea, so-called cardial-ware pottery, marked with the indentations of *Cardium* shells, spread to Italy and Spain, indicating the appearance there before 5000 BC of communities based on farming as well as fishing. To the northwest, the movement of settlers through the fertile lands of

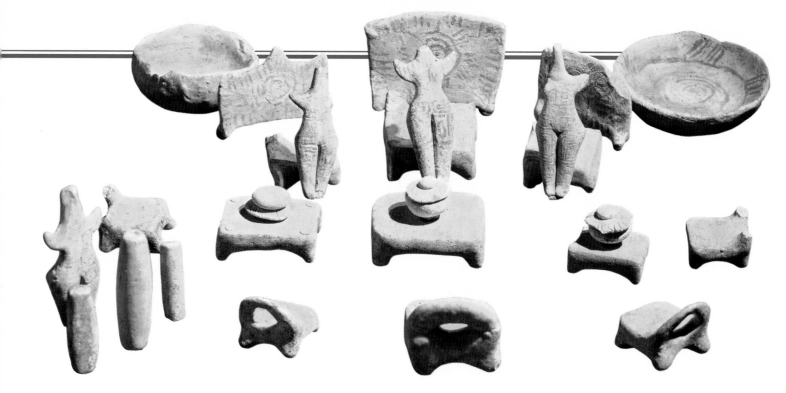

The screenlike items at the rear of this ensemble, found at Targovishte in Bulgaria in 1971, may have served as models of altars at which early farmers sought to ensure the fertility of their soil. These pieces were accompanied by three low tables (center), each of which came with a lidded pot, three cylindrical objects thought to be drums (lower left), and nine chairs, three for each table. (One chair could not be restored and is not pictured.) Of the four figurines, three probably represent girls and the fourth a woman.

the Danube and into the plains and uplands of central Europe can be traced by the occurrence of Linear Pottery, so named for the zigzag or curved incisions with which it is decorated. Soon after 5000 BC, these colonists had established a uniform culture from Hungary to north-central France, and from the Alps to the North Sea.

Within the last half century, scores of Linear Pottery sites have been uncovered across Europe at such widespread locations as Bylany in the Czechoslovakia, Olszanica in Poland, and Elsloo, Sittard, and Stein in the Netherlands. They have provided insights into the lives of Europe's earliest pioneer farmers. The traditional view was that the farmers constantly shifted their settlements, forced to do so when, after having cut down the tree cover and burned up the wood, they quickly exhausted the exposed soil. However, the evidence now suggests that while they indeed used what is known as the slash-and-burn method to clear the land, they founded settlements that proved much more permanent than had been thought. This was particularly the case in central Europe, where the deep, rich loess soil yielded bountiful crops year after year. Archaeologists now estimate that there was enough good land within a reasonable traveling distance of individual communities to support relatively large populations; this meant that people did not have to move every few years in quest of new land.

The Linear Pottery sites differed from those of the Balkan tells chiefly in the construction and size of their dwellings. The villages contained anywhere from two to 15 long houses, the characteristic

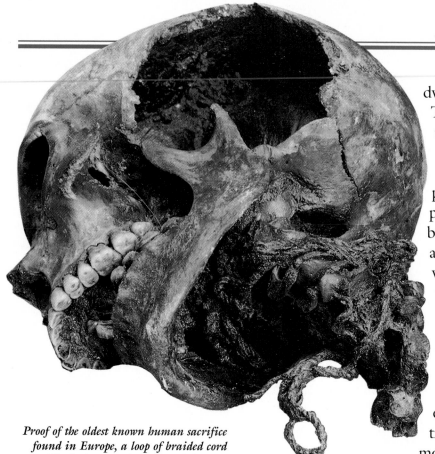

Proof of the oldest known human sacrifice found in Europe, a loop of braided cord still winds around the base of the skull above. Preserved by the coolness, acidity, and oxygen-poor environment of the Danish bog in which it and other bones were found in 1949, the skull belonged to a teenager who lived around 3500 BC. The gaping hole in its side was probably made accidentally by modern peat cutters.

dwellings of the Linear Pottery culture. These great wattle-and-daub structures—in which extended families may have lived—were up to 140 feet long and 20 feet wide; rows of substantial postholes within suggest that upright pillars supported not only a gabled roof but possibly even a loft for storing grain and seeds during the north European winters. Artifacts left behind indicate active trade; among them were necklaces and bracelets made from Aegean *Spondylus* shells.

The pioneer farmers seem to have coexisted peacefully with the relatively sparse native populations they encountered in the dense forests of central Europe. However, as the migrants moved westward, they apparently came into increasing conflict with the local inhabitants. More than 30 western Linear Pottery sites give evidence of having been fortified. At one, Darion in eastern Belgium, Belgian archaeologist Daniel Cahen uncovered intriguing signs of a possible conflict between the two groups. Unlike most other Linear Pottery settlements, Darion's long houses were surrounded by a ditch and a fortified palisade of 500 wooden posts. The settlement had grown up beside a stream; interestingly, no other Linear Pottery sites exist north of this boundary. The stream may well have marked a border with the territory of an aggressive native group, and the villagers might have thrown up defensive structures to protect themselves from attack.

Such apparent boundaries rarely interrupted the spread of Neolithic ways, which were passed on by local adoption of farming practices and by the movement of peoples in search of living room and opportunities. From places like Darion, the Neolithic farmers pushed west until, in the centuries after 5000 BC, they reached the northern peninsula of Brittany and were halted by the gray barrier of the Atlantic. In contrast with the by-now established communities of southeastern and central Europe, these people were pioneers, far removed from the heartland of their culture and entering lands that were already relatively occupied. The coastal regions were home to some of Europe's densest native Mesolithic populations, and as the two peoples met, so the farming lifestyles of one and the semi-nomadic hunting and fishing of the other began to mix. Changes in pottery styles and burial customs around 4500 BC mark the end of the cultural unity of the Linear Pottery style and the growth of regional variations. In time, the interaction between the two communities along what has been termed the Atlantic Facade would give birth to an enduring tradition of monument building that was to last for more than 1,000 years.

Evidence of just when this ancient practice began appeared in 1955, when a resourceful entrepreneur in Brittany turned his attention to a 110-yard-long mound that stood overlooking the English Channel at Barnenez. Finding that the mound was filled with large lumps of rock and good quality gravel, the enterprising businessman began excavating the site and selling the material for road building. Soon, however, the digging revealed not one but a whole series of chambers, hidden deep in the mound's core, and archaeologists were alerted to the find in time to prevent further damage. In all, the monument contained no fewer than 11 separate circular burial chambers, known as tholoi, connected to the outside by narrow passages up to 40 feet long. The French archaeologist Jacques Briard, with a colleague, entered one chamber that had lain sealed for thousands of years. "We had opened up a long gallery filled almost to the top with stones, to arrive eventually at the heart of the monument," declared Briard. "It was breathtaking. The tholos structure was intact. The cir-

Apparently arranged according to strict social rules and family criteria, the skeletons of more than 250 people buried between 3100 and 2600 BC lie in a compartmentalized 36-foot-long common grave at La Chausée-Tirancourt in Somme, France. The image is a composite of 20 to 30 small photographs taken in 1967 by one of the excavators.

cular vault was glistening with a myriad faceted, shimmering beads: drops of water which had condensed on the schist and granite capstones: an unforgettable moment in an archaeologist's career!"

The tombs stood empty, though, the result of the acidic soil of the Breton Peninsula, which ate away the bones. But that barely lessened the archaeologists' excitement. The mound, it turned out, comprised two adjacent monuments of five and six graves respectively, and the burial chambers displayed a remarkable variety of building techniques: Some were made of large blocks of rock, roofed with a single capstone; others incorporated dry-stone walling, with corbeled ceilings. Radiocarbon dating placed one of the two monuments at around 4300 BC; the other was built 400 years earlier, soon after the first farmers reached the Atlantic coast, making it one of the oldest surviving structures on earth.

The impulse that drove western European timber workers suddenly to turn to building with massive stones was universal. Around the time that the Breton builders raised their first stone monuments, the people of northern Portugal were doing the same. By 3000 BC, tens of thousands of megaliths had been erected along the Atlantic and North Sea coasts, from the Iberian Peninsula, through France, Belgium, the Netherlands, Ireland, Britain, and Germany, to the Scandinavian lands of Denmark and Sweden. They took the shape of dolmens, great stone tombs such as the one at Barnenez, usually buried under a mound of earth; or of standing stones, called menhirs, which might be natural or intentionally shaped. The largest of these menhirs, from Locmariaquer in Brittany, once stood 67 feet tall and weighed at least 350 tons, although it has long since toppled and broken into five huge pieces. In most cases, however, the stones are between three and 12 feet tall. Standing stones were also raised in arrangements like the 400-yard-diameter ring at Avebury in Wiltshire, England, which contains within it two smaller stone rings. And at Carnac, on the southern side of the Breton Peninsula, almost 3,000 large stones are arrayed in 13 parallel lines that march across four miles of countryside.

To explain just why early Europeans so quickly adopted stone, British archaeologist Colin Renfrew in the 1970s proposed a theory in which communities throughout the Continent began building independently. Common problems led inevitably to a common solu-

tion—and that solution was stone. The common problems, according to Renfrew, were those of increasing pressure for land. Megaliths are concentrated in areas where the new farming communities encountered the densest populations of Mesolithic peoples. Perhaps, he speculated, the monuments represent the reaction of a native population whose land was increasingly threatened: Highly visible territorial markers not only would warn off potential occupiers but also might provide a sense of continuity and permanence to the community in an unsettled and bewildering world.

On the island of Arran, off the west coast of Scotland, Renfrew surveyed 18 megalithic tombs, set in mounds up to 60 feet long. Because farming on Arran has long been restricted to the coastal lowlands, he was able to compare the sites of the tombs with modern agricultural areas. Renfrew found that all but one of the 18 tombs stand near farmland, and they are so regularly spaced that each seemed to serve its own equal territory and the community who farmed it. A similar careful distribution is clear on the island of Malta, where farming societies raised the world's first freestanding stone buildings around 3000 BC. These so-called temples, built around a series of open courtyards, stand in pairs or in clusters, each relating to one of six territories.

Megaliths must have been more than mere territory markers, however. Some scholars see in them evidence of a cult of the dead. At the entrances to the great stone passage-graves, for example, archaeologists have found signs of offerings as well as animal bones from ritual feasting. Within the graves lay the ancestors of the community—for megalithic burial was more often collective than solitary—and perhaps the practice arose of asking the dead for their intercession with the world of the spirits on behalf of the living. But above all, the great stones were communal monuments, representative of an egalitarian way of life. And after their long heyday, the building of megaliths would eventually cease under the pressure of social change, as the spread of metalworking throughout Europe placed the individual above the community and made the achievement of personal status a goal for those with the drive and means to attain it. But the megaliths would have one final, glorious flowering, on England's Salisbury Plain.

In the 17th century, an anxious reader sought advice from his newspaper concerning a popular superstition. Thanks to the work of the devil, he had heard, it was impossible for anyone to count the stones of Stonehenge twice and come to the same total both times; indeed, it was said to be dangerous even to try. The newspaper counseled leaving the stones well alone. Like 17-miles-distant Avebury, where excavators discovered in 1938 the skeleton of a 13th-century-AD barber trapped beneath a stone that he had been toppling as part of a Church-inspired destruction of pagan monuments, Stonehenge has long been the subject of folklore and superstition. The size of the stones, their isolated situation, and the very improbability of the great lintels raised in the air—the name Stonehenge means "hanging stones"—have invited speculation that can still interfere with mainstream archaeologists' attempts to solve the puzzle of exactly what the monument is, how it was built, and who built it.

Those foolhardy souls of earlier centuries willing to risk diabolic possession by counting the stones generally arrived at a number in the low 90s. Today there are 91 stones, though the original monument probably included around 50 more, arranged in a concentric pattern of four main elements. Within an outermost circle of 30 oblong columns of hard sarsen sandstone that were once topped with an unbroken lintel of 30 more blocks—the enduring popular image of Stonehenge—stands another ring of shorter stones, called bluestones for their distinctive hue. In the center of the circles stood two concentric horseshoe shapes, the outer one made of five massive sarsen trilithons—gatelike structures of two uprights and a lintel—and the inner of smaller bluestones. Around the whole monument ran an earthwork bank and ditch, just inside of which 56 evenly spaced round patches of white chalk, two to six feet across, marked a circle of holes that had been ritually dug and immediately filled in. Interrupting the ring of these so-called Aubrey Holes were four

Seen from the air at right, Avebury may have served as a ceremonial center visited by pilgrims who conducted religious rites within its inner stone circles, only portions of which remain standing. Archaeologists digging there have uncovered axes from virtually every known megalithic area of southwest England, as well as pottery that has been dated about 2500 BC.

standing pillars, the Station Stones, that indicated the corners of a rectangle and may have helped align the circular structures. To the northeast, the entrance to the enclosure was marked by an earthwork avenue, by a pair of individual stones, and by a great unworked boulder, called the Heel Stone, weighing at least 35 tons.

But the bare bones of description fails to capture the impact that Stonehenge has always had on visitors. Evidence of an architectural triumph is everywhere. The towering outer sarsens seem to change color with the weather, from silvery gray to pinkish orange or deep black; these 13-foot-high columns taper toward the top, a technique called entasis that would later be employed by classical Greek architects to give the appearance of straightness in pillars. In addition, the inner faces of the massive lintels are imperceptibly curved to create a smooth circle.

To early observers, even the ruins of such a grand structure could represent only one thing: Stonehenge was clearly a temple. Less clear was whose temple. The conclusion reached by the 17th-century amateur archaeologist John Aubrey and his 18th-century successor William Stukeley has proved as persistent as it is misguid-

ed. To Aubrey, better known today as the author of *Brief Lives,* a collection of sketches of contemporary Englishmen, Stonehenge—like Avebury and other British stone circles—was a temple of the ancient Druids. Known from the works of the Roman writer Tacitus, the long-extinct Celtic religion of Druidism was thought to have revolved around rites involving sacred oak trees, mistletoe, and, possibly, human sacrifice.

Ignoring the signs that no oak tree had ever grown anywhere near Stonehenge, the young doctor William Stukeley enthusiastically embraced Aubrey's theory when he surveyed the site in the 1720s. Indeed, Stukeley went further. Adopting the name Chyndonax and sporting robes, he became a Druid himself. In his book *The History of the Religion and Temples of the Ancient Druids,* published in 1740, Stukeley relegated his long fieldwork at Stonehenge to a mere part of his exposition of a Druid Britain that had been inspired by the teachings of the Old Testament prophet Abraham, communicated to the island race by the ancient Phoenicians. In the despairing words of one modern archaeologist, "He set Stonehenge under a fog-bank of mystification which lasted a century." In the 18th-century popular imag-

Enormous blocks of dressed limestone, the ruins of a temple, stand at Hagar Qim on a promontory overlooking the southwest coast of Malta. Master builders constructed it and at least 15 other temples there and on the nearby island of Gozo between 3500 and 3300 BC—almost 1,000 years before Egypt's Great Pyramid was built around 2575 BC.

The 4½-inch-long terra-cotta figure at right may shed light on the religious beliefs of Hagar Qim's builders. The figure is thought to portray the corpulent Great Goddess, whose slumber may represent the incubation that precedes transformation and rebirth. It was found along with the bones of some 7,000 people at Hal Saflieni, a subterranean burial complex located outside Malta's capital city of Valletta.

ination, Stonehenge became a blood-drenched scene of human sacrifice: Two otherwise undistinguished fallen sarsens were dubbed the Altar and Slaughter stones. Even in the last years of the 20th century, the summer solstice was marked at Stonehenge by small gatherings of white-robed modern Druids who gathered at dawn to welcome the midsummer sun as it came up over the Heel Stone.

The 17th and 18th centuries have no monopoly on fanciful interpretations of the monument. During the 1920s, Englishman Alfred Watkins, a miller and photographer, gained considerable interest with a theory he claimed was born of a vision. Looking out over the Wiltshire countryside, Watkins had revealed to him a network of straight lines that ran across the land like golden wires, intersecting at churches, old stones, and other traditionally holy sites. These so-called ley lines, he insisted, were trackways drawn by ancient surveyors between points of spiritual significance. Poring over maps with rulers, Watkins and his followers imagined that Stonehenge marked an important hub where three major leys intersected, connecting it with earthworks, burial barrows, and even Salisbury Cathedral, some seven miles away. Skeptical archaeologists were quick to respond. They pointed out that the cathedral was built thousands of years after Stonehenge and therefore after the ley lines were supposedly drawn; that one of the lines, a proposed 11-mile track between Stonehenge and the ancient hill fort of Old Sarum, would have unnecessarily crossed three rivers and a mile of swamp; and that there are so many barrows around Stonehenge that it would be difficult to draw any line through the monument that did not align with at least some of them.

Not all unconventional ideas can be so easily dismissed, however. Indeed, Stonehenge continues to prove such an enigma that archaeologists sometimes benefit from outside suggestions, as when, in 1965, American astrophysicist Gerald Hawkins declared the monument to be a sort of Neolithic computer. Using an early IBM computer in his calculations, Hawkins discovered that as many as 24 significant axes between the various stones and infilled holes marked out important astronomical alignments, such as the extremes on the horizon where the sun rose and set during solstices, or the points in the moon's progression across the sky where it seemed to reverse direction. By keeping track of celestial events with movable marker posts or stones in the circle formed by the chalk-filled Aubrey Holes, he believed, ancient astronomers could predict lunar eclipses.

Some of the flaws in Hawkins's argument were obvious. Archaeologists had shown, for example, that the marker holes were more likely to have been offertory pits and in any case had been refilled with chalk shortly after they were dug. But the connection between stone rings and the heavens was taken up by the engineer Alexander Thom. Working from 1955 to 1972, mainly in his native Scotland, Thom concluded that many rings did indeed mark significant lunar alignments when used in conjunction with distant sighting points. Stonehenge itself would have possessed eight such foresights, for which the 16-foot-high Heel Stone would act as the backsight. He identified four of them as earthworks and hilltops visible from the monument, though critics of the theory counter that at least three are far more modern than Stonehenge.

Thom supported his theory by proposing the megalithic yard, a standard unit of measure that is equivalent to about 2.72 feet. He discovered that this shorter yard was used in distances between stones, in the circumference of circles, and in other measurements, not only in British monuments but also in the standing stones across the Channel in Brittany. And where earlier observers had seen irregularly shaped stone rings as flawed attempts at perfect circles, Thom classified six precise geometric figures, including ellipses, flattened circles, and egg shapes, based on an advanced understanding of mathematics.

While Thom's conclusions never gained complete acceptance,

with several skeptics wondering how rigorously he had applied his megalithic yard when measuring sites, a more limited view—that megalithic monuments display solar and lunar orientations—is gaining ground. At the megalithic tomb of Newgrange in Ireland's Boyne Valley, for example, the opening of the passage-grave is aligned to admit to the burial chamber the dawn sun of the winter solstice, lighting up the intricate carvings on the stones within. But just what form such Neolithic astronomy took remains mere conjecture. While some archaeologists detect signs of sun worship, others believe that farmers simply required a type of calendar to measure in the heavens the passage of time and the start of the seasons.

English archaeologist Richard Atkinson, the leading authority on Stonehenge, approached the monument from a different angle. Excavating at the site during the late 1950s, Atkinson had concentrated less on what Stonehenge was for than on the equally baffling question of how it was built. While it now seems probable that the bluestones had a local origin, the sarsens used for the monument do not occur naturally in the region, and at a time when neither the wheel nor draft animals were used in Britain, the Neolithic builders had somehow laboriously transported massive blocks of up to 50 tons across miles of countryside.

The earliest-recorded observers of the monument had no doubts about how the logistical challenges of Stonehenge were overcome: The stones had been moved by magic. The 12th-century chronicler Geoffrey of Monmouth recorded that Merlin, mentor of the legendary British king Arthur, had spirited the stones to Wiltshire from a site in Ireland where giants had first arranged them. Ironically, the tradition of practical fieldwork that was to lead to Atkinson's more plausible answer had been started by the same two men who had done so much to encourage the myth of a Druid Stonehenge.

In the decades surrounding the beginning of the 18th century, John Aubrey and William Stukeley both made scrupulous observations at the site. Aubrey discovered the circle of 56 chalk-filled pits around the perimeter of the enclosure that were later named for him. Stukeley found the earthwork avenue that led down past the Heel Stone, and the nearby two-mile-long elongated earthwork oval that he called the Cursus, or hippodrome, explaining that it brought to his mind the image of ancient Druids enjoying chariot and horse rac-

This gaunt, 17-inch-tall idol from Senorbi, on the Mediterranean island of Sardinia, stands in sharp contrast to the typically rotund female figures unearthed at other Neolithic sites throughout Europe. Such eyeless, mouthless idols are believed to have been regarded as symbols of fertility and nourishment.

65

ing. He was also the first to realize that the axis of the monument, defined by the horseshoes of trilithons and the Heel Stone, is aligned approximately with the spot where the sun rises on the morning of the summer solstice. After Stukeley, a group of enthusiastic 19th-century amateurs led by the renowned gentlemen antiquarians William Cunnington and Sir Richard Colt Hoare not only excavated at Stonehenge but also dug into some 600 of Wiltshire's ancient barrows, which they supposed contemporary with the monument. Sinking trenches across the middle of two or three of the tombs a day, they discovered that the larger long barrows tended to contain more bodies but held fewer grave goods; smaller round barrows were a better bet for finding what Cunnington called "objects of curiosity." For example, in Bush Barrow, a rather large round barrow standing amid a group of burial mounds a mile south of Stonehenge, a single skeleton had been buried with two copper daggers, a bronze ax and lance head, and pieces of worked gold. As Cunnington concluded on discovering some fine, polished black pottery in the hole of a fallen sarsen at Stonehenge, "Our ancestors (if so I may call them) were not so barbarous nor so ignorant of the Arts as some suppose them when the Romans first invaded this Isle."

Puzzled by the two very different types of stone used at Stonehenge, Cunnington and his peers were the first to suggest that the stone circles might date from different times. And 150 years later, Richard Atkinson identified not just two, but at least three main stages in the creation of the monument that stands today—dubbed, prosaically, Stonehenge IIIc. Radiocarbon dating showed that the edifice had been built and rebuilt in increasingly complex forms over a millennium and a half. To the question How was Stonehenge built?, one answer was simple: very slowly.

In its original form, sometime between 2800 and 2100 BC, Stonehenge began as an earthwork bank that was eight feet wide and six feet high and formed a great circle 320 feet in diameter; the entrance causeway was marked by two standing stones and by the massive Heel Stone. At the bottom of the ditch created by digging out the bank, excavators found deer antlers and cattle shoulder bones, the primitive tools that the builders had used to shift the chalky soil. It was Atkinson who discovered that the ring of 56 smallish pits around the edge of the enclosure—the Aubrey Holes—had been dug and then immediately refilled, in what was presumably some kind of ritual ceremony. Around 500 years later, several of the holes

Archaeologists who investigated the Neolithic village of Skara Brae on the west coast of Pomona in the Orkney Islands during 1928 discovered stone axes and knives in shelved storage compartments like those in the far wall of this house, one of 10 in the settlement. Built after 3100 BC, the structures had timber roofs that were likely covered with thatch. The occupants may have been rulers or sages who supervised the construction of huge stone circles six miles to the southeast.

were re-dug and the remains of cremated bodies deposited in them.

But Stonehenge had not yet attained its uniqueness: Similar circular earthworks, known as henges, occur elsewhere in Britain. The complexity of its final form was not even suggested by Stonehenge II, the name archaeologists use to describe the monument as it was when the first bluestones were set up in a partial double ring around 2000 BC. Its construction did, however, provide remarkable testimony to the surpassing importance that the place had assumed in the lives of its community. The 82 bluestones actually include three varieties of igneous rock, which could only have originated from the older geological zones of northern and western Britain. In 1923, the English geologist Herbert Thomas discovered the precise source of these rocks, an area of one square mile in the Prescelly Mountains of Pembrokeshire, on the southwest coast of Wales, some 135 miles from Stonehenge as the crow flies.

During the 19th century, geologists faced with the mystery of how the four-ton bluestones came to Wiltshire concluded that they had been deposited on Salisbury Plain by glaciers during the Pleistocene Ice Age. Atkinson proposed instead that they had been transported 200 miles by boat, along the coast of the Severn River estuary, then up smaller rivers to the Stonehenge site. He backed up his theory with an experiment in which a crew of four schoolboys easily maneuvered a concrete replica bluestone on three 12-foot-long wooden canoes lashed together. But if this was so, why, some pre-

historians have wondered, would the builders have dragged the blocks so great a distance without first shaping them to reduce their excess weight? Moreover, radiocarbon dating has shown that a block of bluestone from a north Wiltshire barrow predates Stonehenge by at least 500 years. In response to such questions, some experts have again turned to the possibility that an Ice Age glacier from the Irish Sea might well have crossed Pembrokeshire, carrying the boulders eastward to discharge them on Salisbury Plain.

However the bluestones arrived, the builders of Stonehenge IIIa a century or two later responded to a new challenge—that of bringing sarsens from a source some 24 miles away near Avebury, then the most holy sanctuary in Britain, and using them to raise the great linteled circle and horseshoe of trilithons. From what Atkinson called "conjecture aided by common sense," he deduced that the stones would have been drawn across the ground on sleds by gangs of workers pulling on ropes, possibly using rollers to ease the task. To set the sarsens in place, some of the original bluestones were removed and discarded.

Such an operation was only possible with a large number of laborers—and with time. Atkinson's own calculations suggested that

Above, an 11½-foot-long stone carved with spirals, diamonds, and other shapes guards the entrance to Newgrange, near Drogheda, Ireland. Sometime before 3000 BC, builders carefully aligned the structure so that sunlight passes through the small rectangular opening above the passageway, along a 62-foot corridor, and into the central burial chamber. The beam, seen at right from inside the structure, illuminates the interior for about 20 minutes on the winter solstice.

moving each sarsen over the hilly Wiltshire Downs would have taken between 1,100 and 1,500 men approximately nine weeks. To transport all 81 sarsens that were used to build Stonehenge IIIa, allowing for interruptions for bad weather and annual harvests, would have occupied a large proportion of the region's population for more than 10 years.

Hauling the enormous sandstone blocks to Stonehenge was only part of the story, however. The sarsens had to be quarried first; this was probably accomplished by building fires in straight lines along the surface of the rock to heat it, then throwing on cold water to produce cracks, and finally driving in soaked wooden wedges that would expand in the fissures and loosen a block. Once at the building site, the stones were dressed by being pounded with boulders. Unfinished tooling on some stones reveals the process: Parallel grooves were hammered into the surface, and the ridges between them bashed out; then the whole surface was beaten level and ground smooth, particularly those faces that would be visible from inside the monument.

The bottom ends of the uprights were left roughly pointed, so that once they were positioned in their foundation holes, using flax ropes and a timber tripod, they could easily be adjusted into a true vertical. First the central trilithons were erected, then the outer ring. Only when the stones had been left to settle into the chalky soil, perhaps for as long as a year, were the lintels added. Quite how these mighty crosspieces were raised on top of the uprights has taxed the ingenuity of archaeologists for many years. One favored theory was that they were carried up huge earth ramps that were later removed. But no sign remained at Stonehenge of the movement of dirt in anything like the volume that would have been required. Then, in 1935, R. H. Cunnington, great-grandson of William Cunnington, proposed an ingenious solution for the absence of any archaeological evidence of either ramps or postholes for scaf-

folding. The builders may have used a large timber crib constructed of crisscross layers of squared logs on which the sarsen rested. By levering first one end of the stone and then the other and inserting wooden supports underneath each and repeating the process to increase the height of the crib, they would have been able to inch the stone to a point where they could maneuver it on top of the upright.

Sometime during the centuries after the erecting of the sarsen posts and lintels, before around 1500 BC, new builders carefully dressed 22 of the previously discarded bluestones and incorporated them back into the monument, perhaps along the line of today's inner horseshoe. For the other 60 bluestones, they dug two irregular concentric rings of holes outside the sarsen circle, but curiously never put them in place. The holes were left to fill gradually with accumulated silt. Then, in the latter half of the second millennium BC, the rest of the bluestones were placed in their present arrangement—in a circle inside the ring of sarsen posts—to create Stonehenge IIIc. One further modification came around 1100 BC, when an earthwork avenue from Stonehenge was extended down toward the East Avon River, probably following the route along which the great stones had been transported.

Stonehenge had changed considerably since its inception. From a basic earthwork henge little different from dozens of others in southern England, it had grown more complex and accomplished until it stood unrivaled. Its development reflected changes in British society as a whole, as new generations inherited and adapted the

Even though Stonehenge's builders used the stone shown lying on its side at left, above, as an upright, two carved hollows, or mortises, indicate that the upright was originally shaped as a lintel. Cone-shaped projections, or tenons, such as the one visible at the top of the sarsen upright above, fitted snugly into such mortises, virtually locking the lintels in place.

Scholars believe that Stonehenge's uprights may have been raised using rope, levers, and earthworks. According to one theory, diagrammed at right, people pulling on ropes dragged the stone up an earthen ramp built at the lip of a ditch (top). Then a lever was wedged under the block and used to tip it slowly into the pit (middle) as the team righted it with a rope and the lever. Finally, stones and soil were thrown into the hole around the base, securing the stone in place (bottom).

monument. The characters in the drama remain elusive, however: So far, no major settlement site has been identified that might have been the home of the builders. Yet from the monuments, graves, and burial goods that these people left behind, archaeologists have pieced together a tentative picture of waves of settlement and assimilation.

In its first incarnation (a simple ditch-and-bank enclosure) Stonehenge stands as the community monument of Late Neolithic farmers. The structure did not exist in isolation, but in the midst of a grassy region already marked as sacred by the earthworks and long barrows of a people identified as the Windmill Hill culture. Named after the site near Avebury where the first henge was found, these were the earliest pioneer farmers to arrive from Europe, migrants who settled among the original Mesolithic inhabitants of the region during the first half of the fourth millennium BC. Such henges have no parallel in Europe, and archaeologists theorize that these monuments were the products of the native population whose contact with the incomers would give rise to what was essentially a new culture. Around the middle of the third millennium BC, however, new practices of burying the dead developed—individually under round barrows, rather than lined up together in a single tomb—among the so-called Beaker people. Named for their characteristic pottery drinking cups, these Britons may have originally been migrants from mainland Europe or just locals who had assimilated the new pottery technique. In any case, it was the Beaker people who also began building freestanding stone circles.

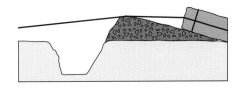

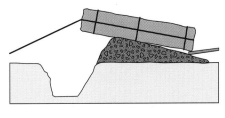

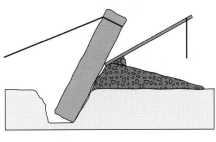

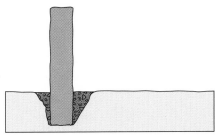

Beaker tombs have yielded rich grave goods. In addition to being buried with their trademark beakers, the dead were frequently accompanied by stone battle-axes and other weapons that reflected the growth of a more martial society. Daggers and knives made of metal also appear, as well as copper beads and pins, heralding the arrival of metallurgy and, in archaeological terms, the dawn of the Bronze Age.

The manufacture and trade of copper and bronze led to new forms of personal wealth that were ideally suited for display and status. The rich burial that William Cunnington had discovered at Bush Barrow early in the 19th century indicated that a new princely caste had emerged from within the previously more egalitarian Neolithic communities. The dead man had been buried with weapons and other objects of surpassing quality. "These were accompanied by a curious article of gold," wrote Cunnington, "which I conceive had originally decorated the case of a dagger. The handle of wood belonging to this instrument exceeds anything that we have yet seen, both in design and execution, and could not be surpassed (if indeed equalled) by the most able workman of modern times." It was set with a chevron pattern made of thousands of tiny gold pins, but, Cunnington recorded, one of the trowel-wielding laborers on his team "scattered them in every direction before I had examined them with a glass."

Born of an emphasis on place and community, the megaliths had served the earliest farmers as focal points, as symbols of continuity, and as links between the living and the dead. Now Stonehenge was entering its closing phase, and archaeologists theorize that the structure that remains today—the great ring of sarsen stones—was built at the bidding of some mighty chieftain. What had begun as an expression of community may have become in its last expression a memorial to an individual, possibly even to the "stout and tall man" that Cunnington found lying in regal splendor beneath Bush Barrow.

The final flowering of Stonehenge around the end of the second millennium BC marked the twilight of megalith building in Europe. Some Continental peoples had never adopted the practice of raising such permanent monuments; they may not have experienced the same pressures or inspirations of the Atlantic coast farmers to demarcate territory, or perhaps they just lacked suitable materials. For the lakeside communities of Switzerland and eastern France—where fish from the lakes provided as important a source of food as grain and fruits and vegetables from the land—life was already settled around a fixed point, the lake itself. Although the vestiges of these settlements are much more modest than those of the monument builders, they are in their way just as eloquent.

The Neolithic village at Charavines *(page 81)*, standing on Paladru Lake in southeastern France, is an unusual archaeological site. The remains of the village lie some 6 to 12 feet under the water's surface, more than 100 yards from the shore. When, in 1972, the local council decided to enlarge a public beach near the site, a group of French archaeologists mounted regular excavations for four to six weeks every summer against the time when the site would be lost to

In this romanticized view of life in a Neolithic lake dwelling, men return from the wild with fish and freshly killed game while other members of the community paint clay pots, tan hides, and enjoy the calm of a primitive idyll. A German artist painted the scene in 1887, after the discovery of hundreds of prehistoric lakeside sites in Switzerland piqued interest among Europeans in what they believed to be their savage but noble ancestors.

the development. Although the lake-bottom operation would be a challenge, requiring the development of experimental underwater techniques, the rewards promised to be great: In the oxygen-poor mud at the bottom of lakes, plant materials and wood decompose very slowly. While researchers on dry land might be left only the outlines of postholes marking the position of a wooden building, Les Baigneurs, as the Charavines site was dubbed, yielded an abundance of actual posts, planks, and beams.

As much as possible, the archaeologists worked in the same way as they would on land, carefully excavating debris layer by layer, and mapping and collecting any finds. Armed with an aluminum triangular frame divided by string into a regular grid that they placed over the area to be surveyed, divers recorded their finds on a waterproof plastic sheet with an ordinary pencil. All necessary digging was carried out with bare hands to minimize the risk of damage. And in order to maintain visibility in the silty water, a current of clear water was pumped through small holes in one of the three-foot-long sides of the frame.

The preservation of organic material that has normally vanished from ancient sites provided a remarkably detailed view of life for the Neolithic settlers who built their village at Charavines around the middle of the second millennium BC, when the site stood on the edge of the lake. Nearby stood extensive forests of beech and fir that provided a valuable natural resource: Wood for building, for fuel, and for fashioning containers and tools such as combs, spoons, and pins, as well as bark fibers for making rope and baskets. The forests also provided fruit, berries, and nuts, sometimes gathered from as far as 20 miles away, to supplement wheat and barley cultivated in clearings. Animal bones show that the inhabitants raised cattle, sheep, pigs, and goats, and also hunted deer and wild boar, while stone weights testify to the use of nets for fishing in the lake.

The long narrow houses of Les Baigneurs lasted for about 30 years until they were abandoned, possibly as the result of a fire, which is suggested by the carbonized planks and charcoal found at the site. Soon afterward, the lake rose to submerge the village for some 20 or 30 years. It was reoccupied when the level of the lake fell but was again abandoned, and sometime later the waters of the lake once more claimed its remains.

The end of the Charavines settlement was echoed throughout Europe by the passing of the Neolithic period. The wood and stone that had sustained the age were to be challenged by metals— copper, gold, and bronze—as a medium for creating objects and ornaments. With the new materials and accompanying technological achievements would come new ways of life that would profoundly affect the farmers of Europe. And, on Salisbury Plain in England, Stonehenge would take its final form as an enduring marker between what had been and what was soon to be.

EXPLORERS OF THE WETLANDS

Some of the most astonishing archaeological finds relating to prehistoric Europe have been made in what might seem the most unlikely of places: sodden areas and under water. But thanks to the airless conditions prevailing there—which restrict oxidation and keep bacteria from destroying perishable materials—objects that would otherwise have corroded, rusted, or moldered away have been preserved to give fleeting but fascinating glimpses of what life was like for early Europeans.

Wetlands archaeology can be said to have gotten under way in 1854 when a drought hit Switzerland's Lake of Zurich, causing water levels to drop and exposing the wood pilings that had once supported huts of a Neolithic village. Archaeologists soon began recovering artifacts from other watery environments, including bogs, marshes, rivers, and submerged coastal regions. Many of the objects retrieved were in excellent condition, not only having survived in an oxygen-poor environment but having been protected by layers of peat, clay, or silt. As more and more wood, textiles, hides, plants, food, animal remains, and basketry came to light, new excavation methods evolved.

Today, one of the most challenging searches involves working in Alpine lakes in winter, after microscopic algae have died and visibility has improved. Since notes must be taken as the excavation progresses, archaeologists use the technique shown in the Lake of Zurich picture above. Here, a diver jots down with a crayon details of the site, an ancient village, on a large, rigid plastic sheet; in the photo lab the diagram will be reduced to one-tenth of its size for study purposes.

Although wetsuits keep the divers' bodies warm as they go about their underwater tasks, the compressed air that they breathe is icy. Three hours is considered the maximum time most divers can endure. "After that, it feels as though your teeth are starting to crack," reported one archaeologist.

USEFUL DATA FROM SOGGY WOOD

Postholes, usually visible as stains left in the ground by rotted wood, enable archaeologists to tell what ancient structures looked like. In wetlands the posts themselves often survive whole or in part, allowing accurate dating through tree-ring analysis, as well as providing details about the buildings. In lakeshore villages, posts and occasional wood floors show that some houses stood above the ground while others rested on piles over the water. Remnants of palisades indicate that many later settlements were walled to protect the inhabitants; such barriers may also have served as buffers against storm-driven water and ice.

The wood recovered can also provide insights into techniques and tools. Marks left on posts often indicate what kinds of axes felled the trees and what equipment was used to split the trunks and make them into planks. At the oldest sites, the wood tended to come from young, pliant trees; at the newer ones, from sturdier, older trees. This fact reflects the available technology: Stone axes were too dull for cutting down large oaks, whereas bronze axes, whose edges could be easily sharpened, were up to the task. In settlements with long histories, an increase in the thickness of the posts is useful in sorting out and approximately dating occupation levels.

The pathway above, woven about 1800 BC from hazel rods, lay hidden under a covering of peat. It once led from a hill to an island in an English bog. People using it were able to keep from getting stuck in the mud.

Beneath the waters of Greifensee in the Swiss Alps, divers use their hands to scrape away a thick layer of wood ash covering the submerged ruins of a Bronze Age village that was destroyed by fire. The site came to light when a number of clay vessels from around 1000 BC were, as a result of erosion, exposed on the lake bed where they had been embedded in the muck. Because the settlement was occupied only once, its single layer offered a clearer picture of the layouts of contemporary Bronze Age villages.

Under a protective plastic hut at a site in Germany's Lake Constance, archaeologists excavate a soggy Neolithic settlement, exposed every winter. In the summer, the melting snow from surrounding mountains elevates the water level and submerges the ruins. Working from raised planks, team members must reach down to clear away the muck from artifacts with their bare hands. To mark the posts they use plastic tags, color coded to differentiate occupation levels.

THE FERRY DISCOVERED UNDER DOVER

In September 1992, at a busy intersection close to the harbor of Dover, England, a backhoe engaged in road construction bit into a 20-foot-deep, water-soaked hole and laid bare a strange-looking piece of wood. Archaeologists who had been monitoring the project could tell, as they cleaned the plank, that it was part of something much bigger. Under pressure to excavate the site quickly so roadwork could resume, they were able, in less than a month, to remove a 30-foot-long, 8-foot-wide section of a wooden boat.

Constructed around 1340 BC—which makes it one of the oldest seagoing boats in the world—and originally some 60 feet in length, the vessel would have required 24 oarsmen. Capable of crossing the English Channel in about eight hours, it may have ferried passengers, livestock, and metals.

The boat was abandoned in a freshwater channel about a half mile inland and gradually filled with tufa, a hard substance that forms in chalky streams. A thick layer of silt then covered the boat as the sea level rose. The presence of pollen, seeds, and beetles in the surrounding soil suggests there may have been grasslands nearby. The skeleton of a salmon found beneath the boat makes it likely that the vessel was abandoned in autumn, when the fish migrate from salt water to fresh.

Archaeologists, racing to reclaim the Dover boat, labor into the night under specially rigged lights and surrounded by a cofferdam to hold back water. To rescue still more of the boat, a second pit had to be dug. The background is lit by the glow of windows and streetlights.

A watertight cofferdam encloses the second pit where a section of the Dover boat is being excavated (top). In front of the dam is the hollowed-out quarter of an oak trunk that formed one of the vessel's sides. This was sewed to the bottom plank by stitches of yew, seen in the inset above. The two planks that form the bottom were joined by wooden crosspieces, and every fourth transverse timber was held in place on each side by a rounded wooden cleat, two of which appear in the center of the photograph (top).

A segment of the boat is lifted from the first pit (left) after being freed from the sediment and placed on a pallet. The vessel had to be cut into 30 pieces for removal. These sections were eventually taken to a specially constructed tank filled with a mixture of water and polyethylene glycol, a water-soluble wax. For the next year, the ancient wood absorbed the wax, which strengthened its outer structure. The segments were further preserved by subjecting them over a 12-week period to freeze-drying, a process that removes moisture.

EXPERTISE OF PREHISTORIC ARTISANS

Artifacts from waterlogged sites often display the ingenuity employed by early Europeans in exploiting their environment. For axes, they chose the wood best suited for a handle. They generally settled on ash or maple because of the hard but resilient wood's ability to absorb shock and rebound, which made the ax more effective. Moreover, these toolmakers used only the strongest parts of the trees, namely the junction of stump and root or branch and trunk.

Bowls too were carved from ash or maple, but a different part of the tree was selected. This may have been a fallen trunk that had already split apart, so that as the wood dried further it would be less likely to crack than pieces cut from a fresh source. Aesthetics apparently played a role at times. A tight burl with a twisted, swirling grain could add beauty to the finished piece while ensuring durability. Sturdy, dense woods, such as boxwood or yew, were also employed to make as practical an item as a comb, whose teeth had to stand up to heavy usage.

Sometime during the fifth millennium BC, a lake fisherman at Knabstrup, Denmark, lost his fish trap (above, right), skillfully woven of flexible plant stems. In those days, fish could also be caught with nets produced on a simple wood frame from linden, oak, or willow fibers. Some of the reclaimed nets, like the one on the right from the Lake of Zurich, are thought to have been used as bags for carrying small items.

A diver brings to the surface a wood-handled dagger still resting on the sediment that has held it for thousands of years. He dug the block out with his hands in order to protect the object until it could be properly removed and conserved. With its handle carefully bound to the flint blade, the implement is typical of the knives discovered at the site, a submerged Neolithic village in Paladru Lake in the French Alps. At right is a sickle fashioned between 1400 and 1300 BC and found in a lake at Fiavé, Italy. The sickle's flint blade is joined with sticky tree sap to a beechwood handle.

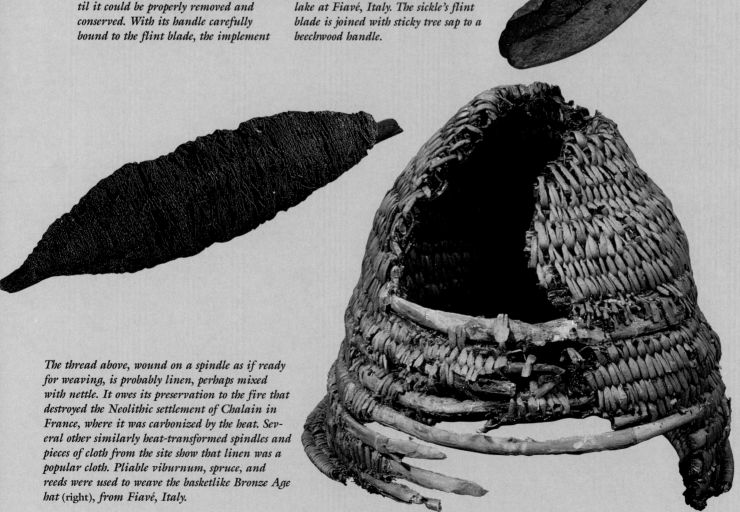

The thread above, wound on a spindle as if ready for weaving, is probably linen, perhaps mixed with nettle. It owes its preservation to the fire that destroyed the Neolithic settlement of Chalain in France, where it was carbonized by the heat. Several other similarly heat-transformed spindles and pieces of cloth from the site show that linen was a popular cloth. Pliable viburnum, spruce, and reeds were used to weave the basketlike Bronze Age hat (right), from Fiavé, Italy.

MESSAGES IN ANCIENT LIFE FORMS

The variety of plant and animal remains retrieved from wetland areas have as much information to shed on early Europeans as their handmade objects. At a Bronze Age settlement site on the Lake of Neuchâtel, for example, laboratories helped the archaeologists to analyze data.

The pollen lab was able to track shifting land use: A decline in the pollen of oaks and a corresponding rise in that of wheat in early levels showed that forests were cut down so crops could be planted, while the opposite sequence pointed to the later incursion of trees into the fields. Similarly, a preponderance of one type of snail and a dearth of another further underscored change, as a moisture- and shade-loving species gave way to a variety better able to survive in open fields. In the dendrochronology lab, cross sections of wood were matched with tree rings dated in previous studies. Thus the years when the settlement was founded and abandoned could be fixed.

The French snail shells, English water beetle, and German moss seen here demonstrate how even small examples of prehistoric organic matter can be preserved in wetlands. From a German Neolithic settlement site, the moss (enlarged at right) was probably gathered 5,000 years ago in the woods and used for house insulation. It still has some of its chlorophyll, visible in the enlargement as dots in the leaves (the circles are water bubbles).

Hazelnuts, shown in the neatly woven basket at left and found in the Lake of Zurich, were a common food of Neolithic Alpine communities. Chewing gum from Germany, still bearing tooth marks, was made from the sap of the birch tree. Its Neolithic enthusiasts apparently believed it had medicinal properties. The charred apples below, uncovered at a burned-out French Neolithic village, had been cut and dried to preserve them for the winter.

DAWN OF THE AGE OF COPPER AND BRONZE

From northern Italy, this seven-foot-tall sandstone stele bears images of Copper Age daggers and axes. An ax of similar design was discovered in 1991 lying beside the 5,000-year-old body of the Iceman, who froze to death in a mountain gully and was preserved under a glacier.

The September sun glinted dazzlingly off the glacier-capped peaks of the surrounding Oetztal Alps as Helmut and Erika Simon began their descent from the 12,000-foot-high Finialspitze. Seasoned mountaineers, the German couple had scaled the tortuous terrain between the mountain's summit and their hiking shelter on the Austrian-Italian border in only a few hours' time. Now, with characteristic daring, they chose an unmarked route across a sloping snowfield for their return, carefully circumnavigating the crevasses and rocky outcroppings in their path.

An hour into their effort they came upon a towering ridge abutting a narrow gully. Glacier meltwater and chunks of floating ice filled the ravine. Skirting the obstacle, they noticed something brown protruding from the slush. "I thought at first it was a doll's head," Helmut later said. They drew closer for a better look and with a startle realized it was the weathered head and shoulders of a human corpse. Near the body was a small, flattened carrying case made of birch bark; close by lay a blue ski binding. From the quaint container and broken binding the Simons surmised that the person had died in a mountaineering accident as much as three decades before.

As it turned out, they were off by nearly 53 centuries. Unwittingly, thanks to the unusually warm summer of 1991 and a layer of heat-absorbing Saharan dust deposited in the Alps by the prevail-

ing North African wind, the pair had chanced upon the freshly exposed remains of a sojourner from the distant Copper Age, a period when Europeans were making the momentous leap from stone tools to implements made of metal. Soon dubbed Oetzi, after the surrounding mountains, by the popular press, the Iceman had lain in a frozen sepulcher for some five millennia, sealed in his protective gully by the massive glacier that glided only a few feet overhead and left his body unscathed.

Scientists have conjectured that icy, desiccating winds accompanying a sudden snow squall had naturally mummified the ancient mountaineer. Now, eons later, he had emerged eerily intact, his dark eyes staring uncomprehendingly at a strange new world. Strewn on the ground about him was a treasure trove of Copper Age artifacts *(pages 113-119),* including a six-foot-tall bow of yew wood, and most notably, a handsome flanged ax of pure copper. (The nearby blue ski binding, it seemed, had simply been lost by a modern skier.)

The Iceman's astonishing antiquity was to go unrecognized for a full five days after the Simons' discovery, however. Back at the shelter, the couple reported their find to proprietor Markus Pirpamer, who in turn notified the police in the Italian and Austrian jurisdictions bordering Oetzi's grave. The next day, an Austrian policeman arrived by helicopter and tried to free the icebound body using a pneumatic jackhammer. In his haste he tore through the cadaver's left hip and shredded the fragile clothing. Fortunately, he soon ran out of the compressed air needed to power his jackhammer.

The reprieve was short-lived. Over the next several days, throngs of curiosity seekers and well-intentioned officials visited the site and, wielding everything from ice picks to ski poles, sought to dislodge the hapless Oetzi from the ice. One eager rescuer used what turned out to be part of the Iceman's backpack frame as a digging stick, carelessly breaking it in two. Another snapped off the exposed end of Oetzi's longbow while struggling to free it from the snowpack. Still others helped themselves to fragments of the wanderer's peculiar-looking tools and clothing as keepsakes.

Only Austrian mountaineer Reinhold Messner divined anything of import in the find. Tipped off by Oetzi's rustic ax and his leatherlike skin, Messner guessed the age of the corpse to be between 500 and 3,000 years old. "As soon as I saw the figure," he remarked, "I knew this was an important archaeological discovery."

Bandied about by the press, Messner's declarations excited the interest of Konrad Spindler, director of Innsbruck's Institute for Prehistory. By then, the Iceman—at last free of his frigid tomb—had been transferred to Innsbruck's Forensic Medicine Institute. Spindler wasted no time in arranging to examine the mummified remains.

After a cursory glance at the Iceman, the prehistorian turned to the recovered belongings. The ax, a wedge-shaped metal blade attached with a thong of rawhide to an elbow-haft of yew wood, immediately arrested his attention. Unable to tell whether the blade was copper or bronze, Spindler instead focused on the ax's advanced design. Unlike more primitive, flat axes, Oetzi's tool had been cast with flanges, or ridges, along its four edges. These permitted the blade to rest more securely in its handle. To Spindler, such a de-

Using this three-dimensional computer model, scientists were able to make detailed measurements of the Iceman's head without disturbing the remains. The studies revealed a brain as fully developed as that of a modern human, and they showed that facial deformities had not plagued the Iceman in life but had been caused by the pressure and movement of the glacier that covered the corpse for some 5,000 years. CAT scans of the body turned up some anomalies, however: Among other things, he had no wisdom teeth and 22, rather than 24, ribs.

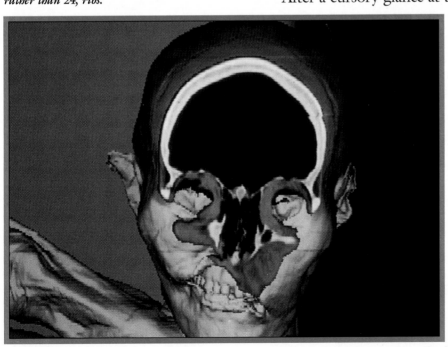

sign—an innovation commonly attributed to the Bronze Age—suggested a time frame for the Iceman of about 2000 BC.

Still, something in the Iceman's wizened form and the crudeness of his possessions seemed to Spindler to betoken an even earlier epoch. He was not surprised, then, when radiocarbon analyses of the Iceman's bone and tissue samples performed at laboratories in Oxford and Zurich registered dates between 3300 and 3200 BC.

What did confound Spindler, however, was the fact that the earliest-known flanged ax of southern European origin, unearthed in an ancient cemetery in Remedello just south of the Italian Alps in the 19th century, had been dated 2700 BC—perhaps as much as 800 years after Oetzi's time. It was as if, quipped one member of the press, the tomb of a medieval warrior had yielded a modern rifle.

Yet the parallel with Remedello was undeniable. Indeed, the same burial that contained the copper ax identical to the Iceman's also included a flint dagger and tanged arrowheads so close in design to Oetzi's as to be interchangeable. Despite the obvious chronological difficulties raised by the match, Spindler began considering the Alpine valleys to the south of the high pass where Oetzi had died as possible locations for the Iceman's home village.

The nearest known prehistoric habitation sites lay in the Val Venosta, an Alpine watershed within an easy day's walk of the Iceman's grave. Although no evidence of settlements remains, graves containing tanged arrowheads and stone axes have produced radiocarbon dates corresponding to the Iceman's era, between 3300 and 3000 BC. What is more, at a place called Merano at the Val Venosta's eastern end, archaeologists have found Remedello-style flint daggers and copper axes, proving that Remedello's influence extended north into the Italian Alps even at this early date.

Still stronger evidence of Remedello culture comes from the Val Venosta itself, in the form of the gigantic picture stones known as statue menhirs. To date, five of these multiton stone slabs, identical in design to those found throughout the Remedello region, have been unearthed in the Val Venosta. Chiseled on each menhir are diagrammatic representations of the human form wearing ornamental belts, and the stones are decorated with images of Remedello-style copper daggers and flanged axes so closely resembling the axes of the Iceman and Grave 102 at Remedello that either could conceivably have been used as a template for transferring the images to stone.

Such cultural correspondences convinced Spindler and other

archaeologists that Oetzi lived somewhere in the Val Venosta, well within the long shadow of Remedello, whose origins now seem to have been rooted in a time considerably earlier than once thought.

Spindler, having settled on a cultural context and home base for the Iceman, began searching for insights into Oetzi's lifestyle. His starting point was the historic culture of the Val Venosta itself. Today—and according to written records, reaching as far back as AD 1240—the peoples of this Italian Alpine region have practiced a form of animal-grazing economy known as transhumance, from the French for "shifting ground." Every June, after the crops have been planted, the Val Venosta shepherds drive their sheep and goats northward through the narrow mountain pass known as the Val di Senales and up into the high pastures of the Oetztal Alps. There they remain with their animals until early September, when they begin rounding up their flocks for the gradual descent to the valley floor. This schedule, timed to avoid the fast-approaching storms of winter, has traditionally placed shepherds back in their villages during the harvest.

That the same rhythms governed life in the Val Venosta 53 centuries before was implied by everything Spindler had so far learned about the Iceman. For instance, Oetzi's death site was found to mark the route by which grazing animals still make their way over the main saddle of the Oetztal ridge to the meadows beyond. And the Iceman's clothing and gear showed him to be ideally equipped for the job of high-altitude shepherd.

Regrettably, such arguments, while persuasive, amounted to little more than speculation. Spindler thus sought additional confirmation from the Alpine environment itself to support his growing conviction that Oetzi had been a herdsman.

He first needed to establish that transhumance had been practiced during the Iceman's day. One particularly salient piece of evidence turned up when it was shown that 6,000-year-old pollen from the boggy plateaus surrounding the Iceman's grave had come from plants that thrive only on well-manured soil. Apparently, under intensive browsing by livestock, the region's natural scrub heath had given way to herb-rich Alpine grasses—a sure sign that Oetzi's ancestors had long engaged in high-pasture grazing.

Similar pollen studies of bogs within the lowland Alpine valleys surrounding the Oeztal revealed the predominance of such cultivated crops as wheat, barley, linseed, and peas. Clearly, the possibility that the Iceman had belonged to a transhumant community was

Discovered in Poland, these copper long-horned oxen from the fourth millennium BC are about five inches long and four inches high. The figures were originally yoked together; similar oxen are depicted pulling plows and carts on 5,000-year-old rock carvings at Val Camonica in Italy and in Germany.

supported by the ancient botanical record. Later, when Austrian archaeologist Markus Egg discovered spikelets of primitive wheat of a lowland variety in the fur tufts of Oetzi's clothing, the supposition seemed all but certain.

Nevertheless, one question remained: If the Iceman was indeed an experienced shepherd—and all evidence seemed to Spindler to point unequivocally to that conclusion—what had caused his sudden death in an area whose dangers he must have known intimately?

One vital clue came from the discovery of a single sloe berry in the icy trough where the corpse was found. A tart fruit of the blackthorn bush that grows thick along the edges of valley forests, the sloe berry ripens only after the first frost of autumn. Its presence among the grave finds fixed the period of the Iceman's death to the waning days of September or the early weeks of October—an interval past the normal highland grazing time. This suggested to Spindler that Oetzi had already made at least one trek to the lowlands where sloe berries abound, a likelihood bolstered by the detection of cereal burnish, also known as sickle shine, on the Iceman's flint blade. The blade had recently been used to cut grain, perhaps during the annual harvest only a few weeks before.

Slowly, a narrative began to take shape in Spindler's mind.

Oetzi, according to long-established habit, had returned with his flock to his village in early September, just in time to lend a hand with the crops. Uncharacteristically, however, he had suddenly returned—presumably, but not certainly, alone—to his high-altitude haunt, now in the early days of Alpine winter.

Aside from this untoward journey into inhospitable terrain, two other factors seemed to Spindler to signify that all was not well with the Iceman. X-rays of the cadaver's thorax disclosed four fractured ribs on the right side. Because the ribs showed little evidence of healing, it followed that the injury had occurred no more than two months prior to the Iceman's death. Stranger still, close examination of the mountaineer's hunting equipment showed it to be in a curious state of disarray. His six-foot longbow of yew—though expertly crafted—was not yet finished. A used bowstring, probably intended for transfer to the new bow, had been stowed separately in a deerskin quiver. And the quiver itself showed signs of disrepair: Its stiffening strut of hazelwood had been broken in three places, and its flap and carrying strap had been torn off. Inside were two broken arrows and 12 unfinished arrow shafts. Apparently, though, he was not carrying enough flint to arm the arrows with arrowheads.

As Spindler saw it, the timing and locale of the Iceman's death, his fractured ribs, and the damaged state of his hunting gear hinted at a calamity of major proportions. Whatever precipitated his flight from the village—whether a personal feud, roving brigands, or an intervillage conflict—it must have threatened him sufficiently to cause him to take refuge in the high Alps despite grim odds.

In the end, his desperate gamble proved fatal. Subsisting on meager food supplies and racked with constant pain, the Iceman was likely in a state of utter exhaustion when a blizzard or a chilling fog drove him to seek shelter in a rocky gully. He propped his ax, bow, and backpack against a nearby ledge and then, drawing his plaited grass cape close about him, lay down on a slab of rock to wait out the storm. Sleep overcame him and he never awoke.

The Iceman's most precious legacy lies not in the details of his untimely death, of course, but in the intimations about his life and the world he inhabited. His was a time marked by tremendous ferment, a seminal epoch in which great crosscurrents of cultural and technological change met and redefined the way that Europeans interacted as well as how they viewed themselves and their existence. It was, no less, a dangerous time. On the heels of change came conflict, both individual and societal. Oetzi's escape into the familiar but forbidding terrain of the Alps is but one measure of the insecurity of the era that followed humanity's long ascent through the preceding Stone Age.

A graphic record of this tumultuous period—known to archaeologists as the Copper Age, or Chalcolithic, from the Greek *chalkos* (copper) and *lithos* (stone)—is written in the statue menhirs dotting the landscape of much of south-central Europe during the time that the Iceman lived. The reliefs engraved on these monumental stones affirm the emergence of three cultural factors that together transformed European life between approximately 4000 and 2200 BC: metalworking; wheeled carts; and the glorification of the human form, which was shown bedecked with weapons and elaborate finery.

The steles' carefully rendered depictions of copper daggers, halberds, and axes, identical to those unearthed in Copper Age graves, betray the fascination of early Europeans for the newfangled craft of metallurgy. In fact, prehistorians believe it may have been humans' love of ornament that led to the discovery and exploitation of copper in the first place.

The blue-green crystals that appear with copper ore deposits undoubtedly caught the eye of Neolithic hunters, who fashioned them into trinkets for adornment or ground them into pigment to use for decorating pots and clay beads. Later, they began to tap the underlying seams of naturally occurring pure copper ore, hammering the reddish metal into beads, wires, and awls for piercing leather.

The next step was smelting, or the extraction of copper from mineral-bearing rock such as azurite and malachite, followed by the casting of the molten metal in stone forms. This advance, archaeologists say, probably occurred serendipitously when a bit of copper ore fell into a pottery kiln, where temperatures could reach 1,900° F. Such conditions would have permitted the copper to separate from the ore, launching a new phase of metalworking in the process.

With copper necklaces and pins came honed knives and axes—ruddy emblems of a vibrant new age. In time, desire for these goods and the raw materials from which they came stimulated the development of major trade routes throughout Europe and ushered in opportunities for accumulating and displaying wealth on an unprecedented scale. A new social order began to emerge.

These trends were helped by the simultaneous appearance, also reflected in the stone art of the statue menhirs, of wheeled vehicles. The oldest European wheel so far discovered was unearthed in a Swiss lake bottom in 1979 *(pages 52-53)*. A solid disk of maple wood, the object dates from approximately 3200 BC, about 200 years after the wheel had made its first appearance in Poland. Wooden wheels like these, when attached to ox-drawn carts, may have granted Copper Age peoples greater mobility than they had known during the Neolithic era, and so allowed for the ready spread of new ideas and technologies. But their real advantage, it appears, was to convey crops from field to storage or to market.

As populations spread across Europe, the first stirrings of a unified European culture began to be felt across the region. All at once, from the megalithic communities of the British Isles and France to the fortified villages of the Danube and the Caucasus Mountains beyond, Copper Age peoples had turned from their millennia-old practice of collective burial to the rite of single inhumation. Individuals who had achieved position and wealth thenceforth tended to be buried alone, ornamented and surrounded by the things that had given them comfort, power, or prestige in life: polished stone axes, copper daggers, copper beads.

By the dawn of what we now term the Bronze Age—around 2000 BC—after prehistoric metallurgists in the Balkans first mixed copper with tin to create the tawny alloy known as bronze, Europe consisted of numerous independent chiefdoms loosely united by trade networks and marriage alliances. In place of the old, more egal-

LAKE HOUSES BUILT HIGH— AND DRY

Swiss antiquarian Ferdinand Keller was the first to examine the ghostly cluster of puzzling wood posts that protruded from Switzerland's Lake of Zurich in the winter of 1853-1854, after a drought had lowered the water level. His claim that the posts were the remains of supports for homes of early Europeans captivated the public imagination.

Scholars too readily embraced the notion of prehistoric peoples living in houses perched on stilts over water. Then evidence from other lakes in western Europe raised doubts about the huts' siting. Academic opinion soon swung to the view that no homes had been built in the lakes, and that piles found under water were there because lake levels had risen since prehistoric times and submerged them.

A 1974-1975 dig on a small island in peat-filled lake Carera at Fiavé, Italy, led to a new view. It turned up an unexpected diversity of Bronze Age dwellings dated about 2000 BC. They were built on the island, on its sloping shores, and also over the water. Even on dry land, the dwellings had stood on piles, no doubt to protect them from rising waters brought on by spring snowmelt and by heavy storms year round.

Posts at Fiavé, Italy (above), *jutting almost 10 feet from the current lake bed, were anchored to an extensive grid of beams set on the bottom; some of these can be seen at the lower right. After the settlement spread from the center of the island to beyond the shore, this substructure was created to steady and protect the huts erected over the water.*

The aerial photo at right offers an overview of the remains of Cortaillod-Est, a Late Bronze Age village at Switzerland's Lake Neuchâtel. Oak piles reveal the outlines of eight rows of houses that were constructed over several decades. The lakeside palisade on the left probably served as a breakwater.

The Neolithic hut, fence, and walkway below were reconstructed at Chalain in France, based on evidence from excavations conducted there and at the nearby lake of Clairvaux. Villages typically consisted of some 10 to 20 such rectangular homes, each walled with timber planks daubed with clay, topped by thatched roofs, and linked by walks of split logs. Wood remains discovered at Chalain were dated to 2974 BC.

itarian communities of the Neolithic and Early Copper Ages reigned a hierarchical society that, much as in Homeric Greece, measured its influence in prestige objects and ceremonial weapons of war. Here and there, petty princes appeared and were interred with sumptuous ritual under towering burial mounds. More often, though, such lavish homage was reserved for the various gods, who were regularly placated with finely wrought bronze swords or exquisitely hewed flint daggers deposited as offerings in bogs or lakes.

Tracking these cultural developments across the stupendous time depth of nearly 6,000 years has been no simple task for archaeologists. With scant exceptions, the Europeans of the Copper and Bronze Ages left few easily identifiable signposts by which to trace their passage. What landmarks remain—postholes from wooden foundations, which themselves disappeared long ago; turf-covered earthworks; burial mounds heaped with mossy stones—reveal themselves, if at all, only as dark depressions or ground swells.

Nor have the archaeological treasures concealed in these ancient formations lent themselves to easy interpretation. Like scholars perplexed by an indecipherable script, today's investigators are constantly searching for a Rosetta stone, a key that will allow them to translate their huge quantities of metal-age finds into coherent history. To date, only a few such guides have been found. One is the rock art of the Val Camonica *(page 92)* in the Italian Alps.

Carved on outcroppings of glacier-polished rock in a hidden valley northeast of Milan, these primitive drawings had for centuries escaped the world's notice. Only shepherds, accustomed to meeting the "fairy scratchings" on their itinerant rounds through the Alpine foothills, knew of their existence. A tip from two such goatherds to a local professor in 1914 brought the carvings a brief flurry of scholarly attention, but they soon lapsed into relative obscurity until 1956, when graduate student Emmanuel Anati arrived from the Sorbonne to conduct a week-long survey of the region's rock art.

For Anati, who found himself mesmerized by the universe of images hidden among the valley's rocks, one week turned into eight years. Between 1956 and 1964, the Italian scholar and a small expedition of helpers identified more than 30,000 carvings, whose provenance ranged from the Neolithic through the dawn of the Latin era—a period of 5,000 to 6,000 years.

Hammered and punched by an early Irish goldsmith, this crescent-shaped neck ornament is of a type known as lunula. Possibly because they were deemed too valuable to be entombed, lunulae have not been discovered in graves but in hoards and other isolated finds.

The finely crafted gold cone seen at left— one of just three such objects ever discovered—was found accidentally in 1844 when a tree was uprooted at a small village in west-central France. The cone stands about 18 inches tall and is thought by some scholars to be a solar symbol. It dates to between 1500 and 1250 BC, the period of the Middle Bronze Age.

At first, Anati could barely make out the figures themselves, much less ascertain their ages. Lichen-covered and badly eroded, the figures initially defied all efforts to impose order on them. But with considerable patience and the aid of dental tools, fine chisels, and water-soluble dyes of varying hues, he was able to resolve what had appeared to be an inextricable tangle of superimposed lines and arabesques into discrete layers of carved reliefs. Later, by noting the design of various weapons, tools, and other objects depicted within each of these separate layers—and afterward cross-referencing them with dated archaeological finds of identical form—Anati assigned time periods to the thousands of drawings scattered throughout the 50-mile-long valley.

Thus organized, the drawings read like a kind of pictorial guide to the psychological and material development of early Europe. In Anati's Period II, for instance, a timespan corresponding to the

New Stone Age of 4000 BC, figures appear singly, often with arms upraised in supplication. Hovering overhead is a schematic representation of the sun—a round disk with a central dot. Here, as Anati interpreted the scene, the worshiper represents both the individual self and the group: The one equals the many.

By the early part of Period III—the Copper Age and Early Bronze Age, between 3500 and 2000 BC—the same scene is rendered differently. The sun, now a rayed orb, shines down on a whole congregation of devotees; each figure stands for only one individual. According to Anati, the concept of the self as an independent entity had thus come into its own.

At the same time, images of sun gods reminiscent of the figures on the statue menhirs make their appearance in the rock art of Val Camonica. Magnificently attired in heavy, metal jewelry and accoutered with copper daggers and axes, these deities have a radiant sphere for a head. Their debut, around the time of the Iceman, heralds the birth of a new materialist ideology based on metal.

Before the coming of metallurgy, most of the rock art was characterized by static scenes of solitary figures shown in apparent prayer or surrounded by beasts. Following the introduction of metalworking, however, humans are shown engaged in a whole array of actions: hunting, weaving, building, plowing, smithing, and driving four-wheeled carts.

By the Early Bronze Age, artists of the Val Camonica had taken to chiseling entire village maps on the smooth rock ledges overlooking the valley. These bird's-eye-view plans—some so faithfully rendered that changeless features of the surrounding landscape can still be identified among the markings—show small, evenly planted fields irrigated by a system of dug wells and surrounded by garden walls. Amid the fields stand clusters of tiny houses flanked by stables and granaries. Fruit trees provide shade.

Also with the Bronze Age came portrayals of villagers toiling in various workshops—the first evidence of widespread craft specialization. There are cartwrights, weavers, carpenters, and—most notably—metalsmiths. In one graphic depiction, a smith is working at his anvil with an apprentice; behind him is a hunter with a shattered spear, presumably brought in for repair.

According to Anati, now a professor of palaeoethnology at the University of Lecce in Italy, much of the impetus for the material and

This rich collection of grave goods was unearthed in an Early Bronze Age burial beneath a megalith at Lannion, France, in 1939. Included in the find are winged flint arrowheads, a large polished stone of undetermined use, copper axes, knives, swords, and a decorative gold box designed to be worn as a pendant.

spiritual revolution suggested by these visual narratives can be attributed to the spread of copperworking throughout greater Europe at the end of the fourth millennium BC. However, this conclusion begs the question of how the first Europeans learned the art of metallurgy—a conundrum that has been debated for the better part of a century. Traditionally, scholars have subscribed to the view that it was imported from the Middle East; after all, the oldest man-made copper objects known—beads, pins, and awls—came from the workshops of Middle Eastern smiths around 8000 BC.

This belief in a Middle Eastern origin for European metallurgy went largely unchallenged until the advent of radiocarbon dating in the 1950s. A decade before, the earliest examples of European copperworking had been traced to the Balkans—to the mountainous, metal-rich lands of Romania, Hungary, Bulgaria, and the former Yugoslavia. Copper punches and beads, along with impressive axes with cast-in holes for affixing handles, were unearthed at the ancient site of Vinča on the middle Danube.

Using dating methods based on comparisons with Aegean copperware, prehistorians initially assigned these objects to a period between the third and second millennium BC—long after their Middle Eastern counterparts. Thus, when the first radiocarbon studies turned up absolute dates of around 5000 BC for the early Balkan awls and beads, and more important, of 4000 BC for the axes, archaeologists were incredulous. Though the Balkan beads and awls still lagged behind those from the Aegean by 3,000 years, the Balkan shaft-hole axes predated their Aegean equivalents by a millennium.

Despite the radiocarbon evidence, scholars remained reluctant to abandon their faith in the primacy of Middle Eastern metalworking. Still more recent findings, however, have all but eliminated such presumptions. In 1968, for example, mining operations in the mountains of Serbia at Rudna Glava exposed more than 20 ancient mine shafts that had been cut vertically into the rock, paralleling rich seams of copper ore. At the bottom of the shafts lay fragments of pottery: large jars and handled vases, as well as what appeared to be ceremonial vessels modeled on animal and human forms.

Serbian archaeologist Borislav Jovanovic of the Archaeological Institute in Belgrade soon identified the pottery as Vinča, from the same site that had produced the Balkan shaft-hole axes dating to the fifth millennium BC. The pottery's presence in the mine works certified Rudna Glava as the oldest copper mine so far discovered in all of Europe or the Middle East. Suddenly, the argument for an indigenous metal industry in the Balkans seemed all but ironclad.

With Rudna Glava firmly set in the Copper Age, Jovanovic went on to scrutinize the available evidence for clues to the miners' workaday routine. To excavate the shafts, he discovered, the workers struck repeated blows to the rock using stone mauls fashioned from large cobbles tied to ropes, remnants of which were found in some of the shafts. In this way, the miners eventually hollowed out galleries as much as 70 feet deep, exposing veins of copper ore along their length. Heavy deposits of soot inside the shafts indicate that the miners built fires against the exposed ore faces. When the rocks had grown hot, they doused them with cold water carried down in their Vinča jugs, causing the stone to contract and shatter. They then used picks carved from red-deer antlers to pry out the ore, which they gathered in sacks for later smelting.

For help in their labors, according to Jovanovic, the workers apparently sought the divine patronage of their gods. Tucked away in a nook of one gallery was a ceremonial vase, from which dual visages of the Vinča mother-goddess peered omnisciently through almond-shaped eyes. Long ago, a Vinča miner had carried her Januslike image with him into the mine, no doubt inviting good fortune in his perilous work. In another shaft stood a tiny, deer-shaped altar with a hollow for burning sacred offerings. Jovanovic believes it may have

Round barrows—mounds of earth and rubble raised over burials of the dead during Bronze Age times—dot a well-tended farm field in Wiltshire, England. Similar monuments are found by the tens of thousands throughout much of Europe, and their contents have yielded much information about their prehistoric builders.

doubled as a portable lamp for illuminating the cramped, inky confines of the gallery.

The willing embrace of such hardship seems to presuppose a compelling social or economic motive on the part of the Vinča, though to date archaeologists have found no evidence of class distinction or conspicuous wealth in the sprawling riverside settlement near Belgrade. Remnants of wooden farmhouses with central hearths and bread ovens bespeak a settled agrarianism, while graves—aside from the ones containing the occasional copper bead or awl—are markedly egalitarian. Yet, a chance discovery at the Black Sea port of Varna some 340 miles southeast of Rudna Glava suggests that the stimulus for the ambitious mine works may have lain farther afield, in the greater Balkan community of which Vinča was only a part.

In 1972, Bulgarian workmen digging a lakeside terrace uncovered a burial pit containing 222 gold objects. Subsequent excavations by Copper Age specialist Ivan Ivanov of the Varna Archaeological Museum showed the grave to be part of an extensive necropolis once associated with a 6,000-year-old coastal trading center on the Varna inlet.

Aside from the timber tracings of a few long-vanished pile dwellings, little of archaeological interest survives of this ancient seaside settlement. But the Varna necropolis, by contrast, holds a veritable embarrassment of riches: Its wealthiest graves together boast the largest assemblage of gold and copper objects found anywhere from so early a date. In one grave, for example, excavators laid bare the skeleton of an athletically built man of 50 who was adorned with

over three pounds of gold finery. On his upper arms were massive gold armrings; around
his neck dangled three golden necklaces. His hair
had been dressed with six small rings of gold and
decorative golden wires had been fastened to his
ears. On the floor of the grave, a shower of gold ap-
pliqué and beads of gold, quartz, and precious
minerals described the shape of what had once
been an ankle-length tunic. Arranged to one side
of the man's body was a polished stone ax with a
golden haft; on the other was a copper spear.
Nearby lay a Vinča-style shaft-hole ax of copper.

Other graves, though seldom so splendidly
furnished, harbored an astounding assortment of exotic treasure: delicate *Dentalium* and *Spondylus* shells
from the Aegean, transparent obsidian blades from the
northern Carpathian Mountains, polished marble from
the south. According to Ivanov, Varna functioned as a Copper Age gateway through which Balkan gold and copper were
exchanged for the wealth of distant lands. This trade in prestige
goods, says Cambridge University prehistorian Colin Renfrew, may
well have played an integral part in stimulating the fledgling metal industries of the Balkans, including the Rudna Glava mine.

*Beaten from a single piece of gold, this ex-
quisite, thin-walled drinking cup with a
separate, riveted handle had been placed
inside an earthenware pot next to the body
interred beneath the Rillaton Barrow
(right). Discovered during excavations in
1837, the cup was later used by Britain's
King George V to store his collar studs; it
is now in the British Museum.*

O
ne thousand years or more
would pass before a compara-
ble industry was to spring up throughout the rest of Europe. This
was, roughly speaking, the Iceman's era—a time distinguished not
only by the widespread appearance of copperworking but also by
sweeping cultural changes. The record of those changes, preserved
in the rock art and statue menhirs of the period, is also reflected
in the grave goods and settlement mounds of the late fourth and
early third millennia BC.

The late Marija Gimbutas, professor of European archaeology at the University of California at Los Angeles, made divining the
pattern of history among these disparate finds her life's work. Beginning in the 1950s, Gimbutas identified certain material changes in the
European cultural record that she equated with major lifestyle trans-
formations during the Copper and Early Bronze Ages.

Most conspicuous among these had been the sudden switch

from communal to single burial, the graves covered by low, earthen mounds, or tumuli. At the same time, throughout northern and eastern Europe, pots decorated with impressions of braided cord made their appearance, along with heavy stone axes. Somewhat later, tanged copper daggers and cord-decorated drinking beakers began to be placed in the grave barrows of central and western Europe. Throughout the Continent, farmers made their way over field and glen in wheeled carts, and stockbreeding became almost as important as planting and plowing.

The uniformity of these cultural trends and the suddenness with which they appeared in the archaeological register struck Gimbutas as more than coincidental. But it was their uncanny similarity to the cultural practices of a Neolithic tribe of cattle herders from the Russian Steppe that most intrigued her. These itinerant stockbreeders—known as the Kurgan people for their habit of interring their ocher-sprinkled dead singly under earthen tumuli, or kurgans—were among the first prehistoric people to domesticate the horse and to use four-wheeled carts. Moreover, they embellished their pottery with cord designs made by pressing hempen ropes into the freshly modeled clay.

The weed-choked entrance to the cist, or stone-lined burial chamber, of the Rillaton Barrow in Cornwall belies the rich grave goods that were found there in 1837. In addition to the delicate gold vessel at left, a fine bronze dagger, pieces of bone, and beads lay alongside the tomb's male occupant.

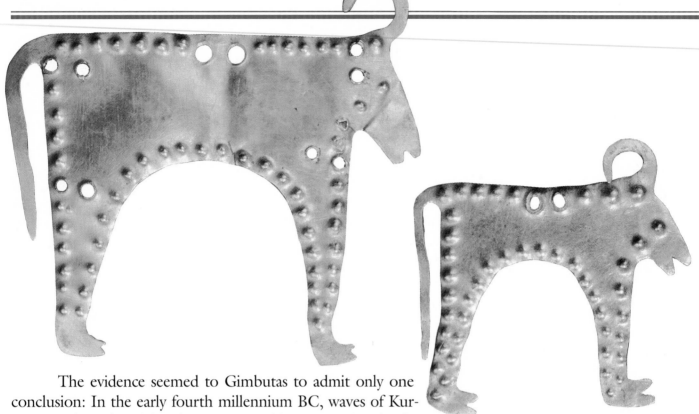

The evidence seemed to Gimbutas to admit only one conclusion: In the early fourth millennium BC, waves of Kurgan invaders—lured by the promise of better grazing lands or wanderlust—began spreading west from their Russian homeland. Traveling by horse and cart into the vast European fastness, they introduced new cultural traditions and a more mobile way of life.

The course of 500 years was to witness four separate Kurgan invasions, each of which would leave its distinctive imprint on the material record. The last of these, Gimbutas maintained, was to prove the most influential: Sometime during the early third millennium, bands of horse-mounted Kurgan archers swept into the ore-rich lands of the Balkans, where they learned from local metalsmiths how to smelt ore and fashion copper knives and axes. Then, carrying their newfound knowledge with them, they made their way along the Danube into the forested heart of Europe. Their characteristic drinking cups—tall, thin-walled, handleless beakers, colored red or black and incised with geometric shapes and decorative cording—would earn them the archaeological designation of the Beaker people.

The first evidence of Beaker infiltration in Europe had been discovered in England a full century before Gimbutas began her provocative work on the prehistoric cultures of the Copper and Bronze Ages. Sometime during the 1850s—inspired by the sight of two Stone Age skulls at a nearby medical institution—Wiltshire physician and brain specialist John Thurnam suddenly developed a

Dating to about 4000 BC, this pair of bulls formed from sheet gold was found with numerous other gold objects in a prehistoric burial site at Varna, Bulgaria, in 1972. The smaller of the two animals measures about 1½ tall, the larger a little more than 2¼ inches. Both were probably sewed onto clothing for ornamental effect.

Still gripping the shaft of a golden scepter, a well-preserved male skeleton from the Varna cemetery lies, ankles crossed, amid copper axes and other grave goods. Clearly visible are the many gold ornaments that once embellished the body and adorned the long-disintegrated burial robes and headdress.

These thin-walled, artfully produced pottery vessels are among thousands recovered from graves and dwelling sites of the British Isles's so-called Beaker people, who flourished between 2500 and 2000 BC. The pots are decorated with characteristic strips of geometric patterns alternating with plain bands.

keen interest in prehistoric archaeology. Casting about for a suitable object of study, Thurnam settled upon the barrows of Britain—the hundreds of turf- and stone-covered burial mounds scattered throughout the English countryside *(page 101).*

The barrows, he soon discovered, took one of two forms: oblong mounds over multiple burials inside megalithic crypts, and round mounds over smaller, individual burial pits. The long barrows he rightly attributed to the Neolithic period. The round barrows he guessed to be younger. It was these that would absorb his attention for the next 20 years

Beneath the bowl-shaped mounds, each encircled by a ditch, Thurnam unearthed the remains of a class of powerful bowmen. Besides the hallmark Beaker ware, the male burials typically contained the full complement of archer's regalia: finely chipped flint arrowheads; a wristguard—a curved rectangular plate of stone, bone, or baked clay attached by bronze rivets and gold studs to a leather strap—used for protecting the left arm against the snap of the bowstring; and a broad-bladed dagger of copper, bronze, or flint. In a few burials, hawks' heads suggested falconry. Also in evidence was a love of finery: One young archer, exhumed near Oxford, wore gold earrings and the remains of a delicately woven tunic of nettle fiber.

Neuroanatomist that he was, Thurnam could not help noting one additional detail: The craniums of the Beaker people were rounded, whereas those of their Neolithic predecessors were long and narrow. "Long-barrows, long skulls; round barrows, round skulls," became a scholarly catch phrase of the day. Thurnam interpreted these marked differences in physical type as racial. Taller and more powerfully built than the megalith builders, the Beaker people seemed ideal candidates for an invasion force.

Later investigators found little or no trace of armed struggle, however, and only meager evidence of settlement. In Downton and Dartmoor in southern England, for example, archaeologists detected the postholes of skin tents and the foundations of ramshackle stone huts that—to judge from associated sherds of Beaker pottery—may once have housed these elusive nomads. Apart from cattle herding and sheepherding, the Beaker people were speculated to have devoted a good deal of their time to beermaking and beer drinking. In support of this view, researchers cited the ubiquity of the elegant drinking beakers, one of which was found to contain a few telltale grains of fermented millet.

Before long, Thurnam's round barrows began attracting worldwide attention. In 1912, Swedish archaeologist Nils Aberg raised the Beaker people from the status of an obscure British tribe to that of a European phenomenon with the announcement that Beaker-style burials had been found not only in Brittany but in southern France, Holland, Switzerland, Spain, the Rhineland, and Denmark as well. Subsequent probes turned up Beaker paraphernalia in barrows in the Shetland Islands, Ireland, Sicily, Sardinia, Portugal, and Poland. The uniformity of the Beaker finds and the apparent rapidity with which Beaker ware had spread throughout central and western Europe gave

Known as the Folkton Drums, these unique, carved chalk cylinders were found in the otherwise undistinguished grave of a child near Folkton, in England's Yorkshire. Along with their geometric designs, the drums feature a distinctive eye-and-eyebrow motif. The largest of the objects measures nearly six inches across.

rise to the notion—championed by renowned archaeologist V. Gordon Childe—that the Beaker people were armed bands of tinkers and traders who had journeyed about the Continent on muleback, exchanging precious metal objects and beer for amber, jadeite, and jet.

Around the same time that the Beaker people were achieving fame as pan-European travelers, another group of prehistoric itinerants captured the notice of the archaeological community. One of the first to pay them formal attention was Danish archaeologist Sophus Muller, who spent the last three decades of the 19th century systematically cataloguing the grave goods of a series of round barrows—known colloquially as fairy hills—dotting the landscape of Denmark.

The burial customs in at least half of the barrows followed a distinct pattern: Women lay on their left sides with their heads pointing east, men on their right sides with their heads to the west. Around the perimeter of the grave pit stood cord-decorated pottery. A strand of amber beads sometimes dressed female corpses. Frequently, however, the gaze of the men was directed toward the butt end of a splendid battle-ax of finely cut and polished stone.

More than mere weaponry, such axes were symbols of power and prestige. Many, in fact, imitated in shape and detail the coveted copper and bronze axes of the south and west, right down to the seams left by the casting process. There in the metal-poor north, craftsmanship made up for a dearth of ore.

Soon, similarly furnished burials were identified along a broad arc stretching from Scandinavia through central Germany, Poland, Slovakia, and central Russia. The grave inhabitants, loosely styled the Corded Ware people—after their custom of decorating pottery with impressions of twisted cord—were regionally known by the aliases Battle Ax people, Single Grave people, and Ocher Grave people, according to local whim.

During the mid-20th century, a number of noted prehistorians—Marija Gimbutas among them—coined elaborate theories accounting for the origins and movements of both the Corded Ware people and the Beaker people. They did this, by and large, by interpreting stylistic changes in each group's respective pottery types, afterward organizing them into datable sequences.

Ever since, heated debates have raged over whether these mobile bands got their start in the east, on the distant Russian Steppe or in the Balkans; or in the north, in Scandinavia; or even perhaps in the west on the Iberian Peninsula, which comprises modern-day

Found beside the skeleton of a man buried under a mound in Leubingen, Germany, this collection of gold jewelry includes a large torque, or neck ornament, a pair of earrings, two pins for fastening clothing, and a spiral bead. The grave, dating to about 1900 BC, was excavated in 1877.

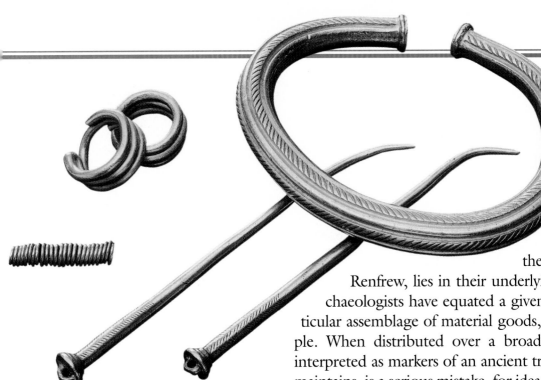

Spain and Portugal. As yet, however, not one of the proposed scenarios—Gimbutas's Kurgan theory included—can be confirmed by available dating evidence.

The problem with all these speculations, says Colin Renfrew, lies in their underlying premise: Traditionally, archaeologists have equated a given pottery form, or even a particular assemblage of material goods, with a specific group of people. When distributed over a broad area, such finds have been interpreted as markers of an ancient tribal migration. This, Renfrew maintains, is a serious mistake, for ideas and cultural trends may have been passed between communities through trade and other interactions, with no concurrent movement of population.

According to British archaeologist Stephen Shennan, the Corded Ware and Beaker traditions that transformed European culture during the third millennium BC were not the legacy of foreign invaders. Rather, they represented the adoption by certain native elites of fashionable practices and prestigious objects recognized throughout Europe as conferring high status.

Thus the handleless drinking cups and riveted bronze knives of the Beaker people, and the polished stone axes and fine-tempered pottery of the Corded Ware people, may be seen as straightforward symbols of status, used and displayed for the self-aggrandizement of the upwardly mobile. Such so-called status kits, as well as many of the technological and social changes that attended their appearance, could have been transmitted through Europe in a relative twinkling, passed on through a simple chain of local interactions.

Whether viewed as the bequest of enlightened invaders or as the tokens of a social and economic revolution, the changes associated with the Corded Ware and Beaker traditions were very real. Now true elites began to develop, and individuals, jockeying for position in a society newly ranked by opportunities to amass material wealth, turned increasingly to one-upmanship and ostentatious display as the egalitarian bonds of community gave way to unbridled competition.

Nowhere was this new social order more in evidence than on the cliff-girt coasts of Brittany and southern England, where, begin-

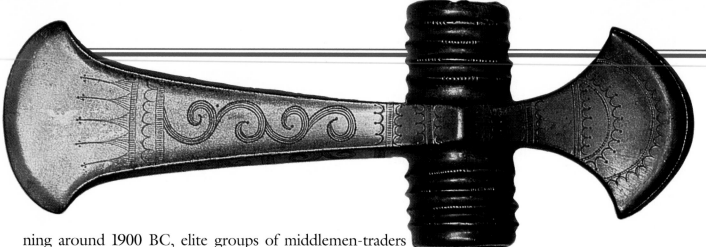

ning around 1900 BC, elite groups of middlemen-traders erected ephemeral commercial kingdoms.

Today these petty magnates are remembered only for their imposing burial mounds—those great round heaps of turf and stone rising some 30 feet above the surrounding plain and stretching 100 feet across. Among the most extraordinary of these is the burial at Kernonen en Plouvorn in northwest Brittany, discovered in 1961. Acid conditions in the stone-lined chamber had destroyed any evidence of human remains, but three crushed oak coffers were found, each brimming with rich burial goods. Inside were four flanged axes of bronze, 60 flint arrowheads, an archer's wristguard fashioned from amber, the scattered beads of an amber necklace, bronze pins, a bronze dagger with a carved bone pommel, and three bronze daggers still in their scabbards of bark and hide. Careful examination of the wooden hilts of the bronze daggers revealed intricate geometric designs, hammered in thousands of minuscule gold nails. Approximately 5,000 of these glittering pins—none bigger than an eyelash—had been used to adorn each weapon.

French archaeologist Jacques Briard attributes the flowering of these western European aristocracies to the commercial talents of their chiefs, who displayed a notable flair for managing the region's considerable metal resources and conducting the intercontinental trade that grew up around them. Cross-Channel traffic in Irish gold, Cornish tin, and British copper, for example, was probably carried out using small wooden or skin boats, prehistorians say. On a good day, these doughty craft would have made the trip from England to Brittany in only four to five hours. Once ashore, Wessex traders could have exchanged their precious metals for exotic riches like Baltic amber and blue Egyptian glassware.

Such luxury trading, stimulated in large part by the burgeoning metal industry of the Early Bronze Age, in turn fueled the advance of European metalworking itself. As demand for copper and bronze commodities rose, pioneering centers of metallurgy grew up,

Thought to have been part of a votive offering, the lavishly decorated bronze battle-ax above is one of 12 such weapons retrieved from the opulent Hajdusamson hoard at a site in northeast Hungary in 1907. The axes, their cutting edges facing to the west, were laid out along the blade of the finely crafted sword at right, whose tip pointed resolutely to the north.

supported by thriving communities of farmers, stockbreeders, warriors, prospectors, miners, smiths, and traveling merchants.

By 1800 BC, a powerful nucleus of metalworking and trade had emerged in central Europe, embracing parts of present-day Austria, Germany, and Hungary. From workshops in the rolling hills of Bohemia, virtuoso smiths were turning out metalworks of exceptional quality and beauty: fine flanged axes, spiral bracelets, triangular bronze daggers chased with intricate designs, droplet earrings, and ring-headed pins. Archaeologists refer to this culture as Únětice, after a prehistoric necropolis a few miles northwest of Prague, where a local doctor unearthed a cache of such metalworks during the late 19th century.

Ideally positioned to exploit not only its own Bohemian tin resources but Balkan and Alpine copper as well, the Early Bronze Age peoples of the Únětice culture also controlled the amber routes that connected the Baltic with the Mediterranean. Not surprisingly, a Wessex-style chiefdom soon arose in Únětice Saxony, where a handful of enterprising potentates succeeded in diverting some of the wealth of the Bronze Age to their own coffers.

Like their western-European counterparts, the Saxon elites of Únětice had themselves interred under enormous tumuli. But a few, at least, seem to have taken the princely funeral regimen a step further: In one particularly grandiose burial in Leubingen *(page 109)* in eastern Germany, 19th-century excavators discovered the skeleton of a child ceremonially laid across the lap of an old man. Jiri Neustupny, dean of Czechoslovakian archaeology, believes that the child was a servant girl who had been ritually sacrificed to accompany her august master on his journey to the sun god.

In life, the patriarch of Leubingen may have earned his wealth and fame as a master metalsmith. Along with a cushion stone for metalworking, diggers found a carpenter's tool kit and a vast collection of weapons and ornaments—axes, halberds, and daggers; and a massive torque, or necklace—of rolled gold, not unlike the martial finery that is depicted on the statue menhirs of the Copper Age.

The discovery of smith's equipment in several affluent Únětice burials has led some archaeologists to conjecture that, at least in this sophisticated metalworking culture, smithery had been elevated to an elite art.

The prestige attending Únětice metalwork was enormous. Coveted by traders as far away as the eastern Baltic, Scandinavia, and the British Isles, it inspired the birth of copycat industries in Bavaria, Switzerland, and France. And to the east, in the Carpathian foothills of Transylvania, it sparked the development of a rival school of metallurgy whose distinctive wares blended the best of Únětice technological know-how with new, visionary designs. These were the works of the renowned Otomani smiths, named for a Bronze Age settlement unearthed in northwest Romania in 1924.

With the Otomani metalworkers, the art of European metalcraft reached its apogee during the mid-second millennium BC. Never before or after were so many splendid daggers, battle-axes, swords, and halberds to issue from the workshops of prehistoric smiths.

Of these, the most famous examples are from a find known as the Hajdusamson hoard *(pages 110-111)*, a collection of richly ornamented weapons uncovered in a drainage works in the sandy plains of northeast Hungary in 1907. Carefully arranged in an earthen pit, the hoard comprised a bronze-hilted sword, with its blade pointing due north and lavishly incised with whorls and spirals, and 12 shafthole battle-axes oriented to the west.

The purposeful placement of the weapons and their exquisite craftsmanship suggest a votive function for this buried treasure. Perhaps the weapons had been offered with great ceremony by an Otomani chieftain anxious to influence the outcome of some conflict by pleasing the gods.

Such musings are not beyond the realm of possibility, archaeologists say. For the new social order of the Middle Bronze Age—with its emerging warrior elite and its growing stake in the luxury trade—brought with it dangerous times. Otomani and Unetician peoples increasingly withdrew to the naturally defensible slopes of hills, promontories, and high riverbanks, erecting their sturdy timber dwellings inside protective earthen ditches and wooden palisades.

In these developments can be seen the beginnings of a time that seems to modern society much like the heroic age of later Greek legend, in which petty chieftains and warriors passed their days in plundering raids and in hunting, feasting, and boasting of their worth. Out of such vainglorious pursuits would grow a new Europe, infinitely more complex and rivalrous than the one before.

A MAN FROZEN IN TIME

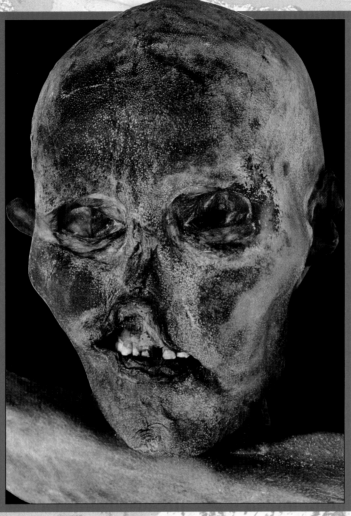

When found, the 5,000-year-old Iceman lay face down in a gully in the Tyrolean Alps on the border between Austria and Italy *(background)*. Researchers believe that, weakened by four recently broken right ribs, he died of exposure. As snow covered his body and equipment, winds whipping through the mountains essentially freeze-dried the corpse, mummifying it. The depression that became the Iceman's tomb prevented his remains from being torn apart by the glacier that flowed over them; only his nose and upper lip *(above)* would be disfigured by ice.

Had it not been for an unusual warming trend in 1991 that shrank the glacier, the Iceman might never have been found. Racing against worsening weather, scientists labored for six days to free the body and salvage apparel, tools, and equipment. Not until a year later could they return for a second search. After spending three weeks carting off 600 tons of winter snow and ice, they retrieved more remnants of clothing and gear, as well as human tissue, hair, and a fingernail.

Subject to intense scrutiny in the Austrian laboratory where he came to rest, the Iceman has slowly yielded his secrets. The experts have been able to come up with his medical history using x-rays, computer tomography scans, and internal probes, and they have determined details of his daily life. How he broke his ribs no one knows, but he seems to have been running away from something or someone. He ventured into the mountains with his quiver strap broken, his bow unfinished, and his 14 arrows useless. Moreover, he seems to have lost his pyrite, or firestone, used for igniting tinder. Down on his luck, he apparently ate a meal of dried ibex meat (as suggested by bone fragments on the ground), then lay down on his left side to take the pressure off the painful right, grew drowsy from hypothermia—and entered the sleep of centuries.

PROBING FOR THE ICEMAN'S PAST

Radiocarbon dating of tissue samples from the Iceman confirmed that he lived between 3300 and 3200 BC, in the Copper Age, and DNA tests proved him to be an ancestor of contemporary central and northern Europeans. As indicated by the wear on his cavity-free teeth and scans of his body, he must have been 30 or so years old when he died. Still, the Iceman displayed signs of aging. His arteries were already beginning to harden, and he suffered from the early stages of arthritis.

To avoid contaminating the corpse as they examined it, scientists used instruments made of titanium rather than of alloys, which might have left traces of lead, cadmium, and iron. Hair analysis showed low lead levels in the body, pointing to the purity of the Iceman's environment. Yet as one doctor watched a monitor during an endoscopic probe of the Iceman's internal organs, he was surprised to see how black the lungs were—a sign that the Iceman had spent much time in a smoky interior.

Grain found in his clothing and among his paraphernalia tie the Iceman to an agricultural community and a late-summer harvest. It is likely he was a shepherd; indeed, his body was discovered where herds of goats and sheep still cross ancient Alpine trails on their way to high pastures for summer grazing.

For first aid, the Iceman had with him these two pieces of birch fungus threaded onto fur strips. Folk medicine has long applauded the antibiotic uses of tree fungi as a treatment for, among other things, bladder ailments and tuberculosis. A sloe berry found in the Iceman's vicinity suggests he may have carried the vitamin- and mineral-rich fruit for health reasons.

The Iceman's body retains the pose in which it was found. Although he died stretched out on his left side, pressure from ice and snow turned him face down, forcing the left arm that had extended in front of him across his shoulders. Researchers estimate that the Iceman was five feet two inches tall.

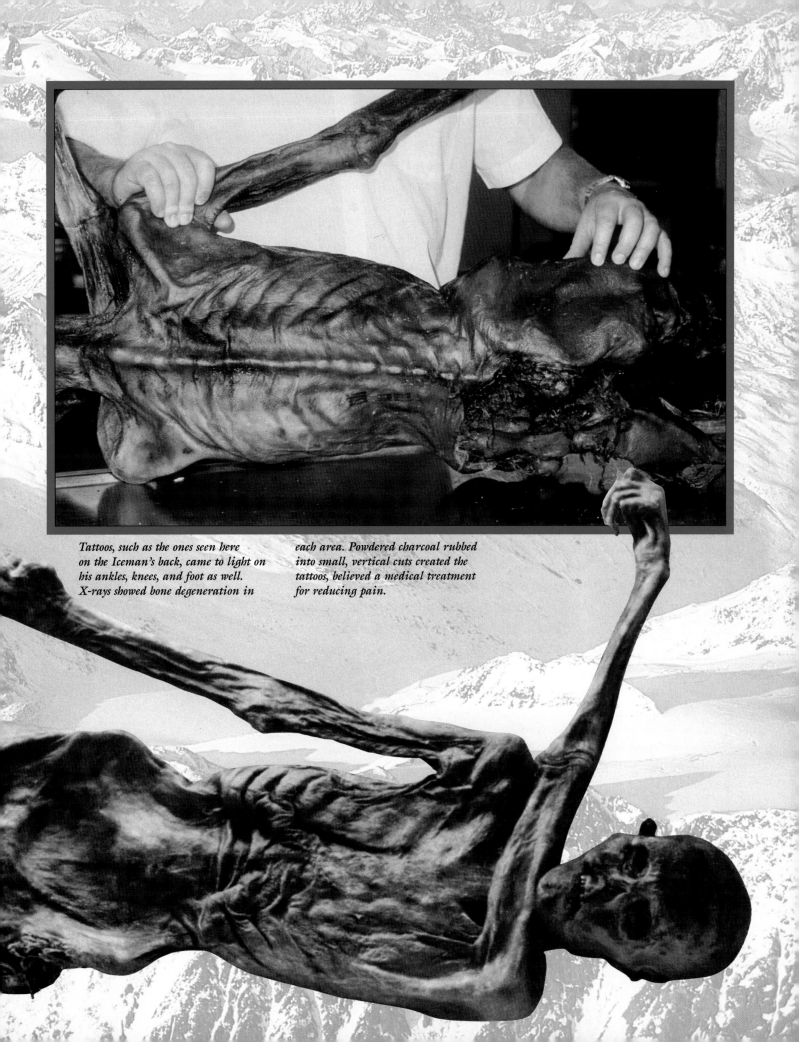

Tattoos, such as the ones seen here on the Iceman's back, came to light on his ankles, knees, and foot as well. X-rays showed bone degeneration in each area. Powdered charcoal rubbed into small, vertical cuts created the tattoos, believed a medical treatment for reducing pain.

OUTFITTED
AGAINST THE
ELEMENTS

From the hat that warmed his head to the shoes that protected his feet from frostbite, the Iceman was dressed for the mountains. His shirt *(not shown)* was fashioned out of many small, square, fur pieces sewed together to guarantee a snug fit. Both sides showed considerable wear, suggesting that in winter the Iceman may have worn the fur side against his skin and reversed the shirt in summer.

The Iceman hoisted his loose-fitting fur leggings with fur straps that fastened to a pouch tied around his waist. He pushed fur flaps attached to the bottom of each legging well into the top of his shoes, protecting his lower legs from invading wetness as he trod through snow.

A soft leather loincloth covered more than the Iceman's genitals; he pulled the front flap up and over the pouch, protecting its fire-making contents from moisture. But a tear in the front may explain why his firestone and the flint he struck it against to make sparks were missing.

Consisting of plaited bundles of long grass (above), the Iceman's cape kept him dry in rain. The garment may also have served as a sleeping mat, a blanket, and camouflage on hunting expeditions. Dressed in the attire he wore when he died, the Iceman is depicted here in a sketch by artist Julia Ribbeck of the Römisch-Germanisches Zentralmuseum in Mainz, Germany, where experts restored and conserve the artifacts. Although only four hairs survived on his body, he is shown here bearded; researchers believe he had wavy black hair.

The Iceman's cone-shaped hat, made from small fur patches stitched together, has two leather strings that form the chin strap. A fragile covering of fur still clung to its outer side when it was retrieved during the second recovery period, in August 1992.

Stuffed with clumps of grass for warmth, the Iceman's shoes (below) may have been crafted by his own hand. Cowhide soles are bound to fur uppers with strong leather straps. Inner socks made from twisted and knotted cord form nets that hold the grass in place. The right shoe—better preserved than the left one—was still on the Iceman's foot when his body arrived at the laboratory.

117

With a flint blade as small as an arrowhead (near left), *the Iceman's dagger seemed too tiny to serve much purpose. Yet microscopic analysis showed traces of blood; he had used the knife in his last days to butcher meat. The dagger fits neatly into the accompanying scabbard (far left), made from linden-tree fibers. Ripped by an ice pick during recovery, it is considered by experts an outstanding example of early plaiting technique.*

The pouch below, worn like a belt around the Iceman's waist, contained several items for making fire and doing work. At the bottom, far left, is tinder fungus. Just above it is a bone awl for stitching leather. To the right of the awl are three flints. The largest apparently served the Iceman as a sickle, allowing him to cut grass to stuff into his shoes as insulation. He used the smaller, pointed one to drill holes in wood. And the tiniest enabled him to carve shaft slits for arrowheads. To the right of the flints, the pencil-like object tipped with a splinter of stag antler is a retoucher, which the Iceman wielded to give his flint tools a sharp edge.

Covered with a rust-colored patina produced by water, the blade of the Iceman's ax was thought to be an iron one by initial observers and misled them into believing that his remains were anywhere from 500 to 3,000 years old. But x-rays showed that the ax was made of copper, dating it before the Bronze Age. And microscopic analysis showed that during his last days the Iceman worked at reseating the ax head into its handle, employing birch tar—prepared by prolonged heating of birch bark—as glue.

Exposed as the ice melted, this birch-bark vessel lay in fragments on a rock ledge where its owner had placed it. Specialists in Mainz steamed the warped pieces to make them supple enough for reshaping. A similar receptacle found near the Iceman's head—apparently the last object he grasped—once contained live embers for fire making. Its blackened interior still held grass and charcoal, along with green maple leaves for wrapping around the embers to keep them from dying.

The contents of a fur quiver offer insights into the Iceman's last days. Although two of the arrows bore points, they were broken; the other 12 arrows were mere shafts. Their lack of readiness—along with the unfinished state of the bow—is part of the evidence that suggests a hasty, unplanned departure from home for the Iceman. Further clues are provided by the quiver itself: Not only its strap but its supportive wood strut were broken, which meant it had to be carried by hand. Its cap was missing too, presumably lost.

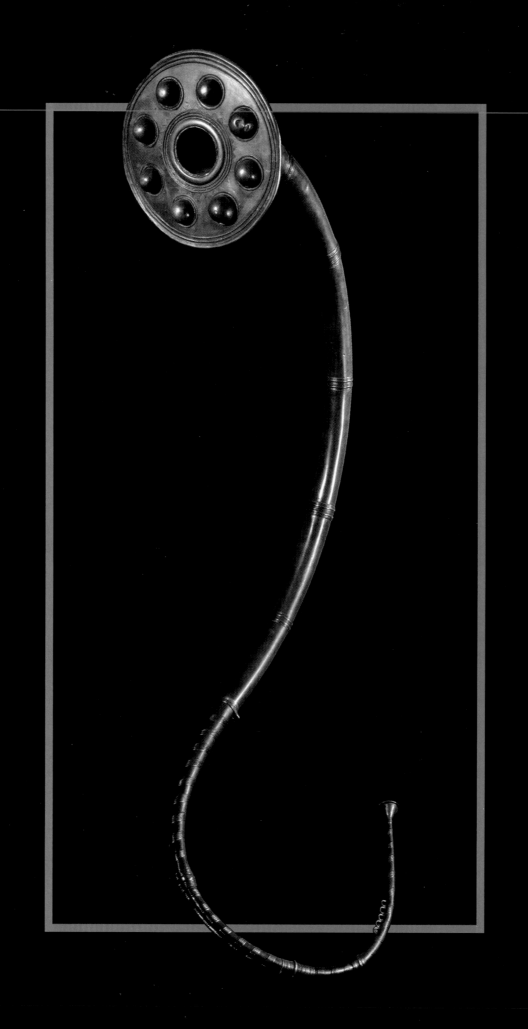

TENSION AND STRIFE IN A NEW SOCIETY

The lur, a bronze horn whose tone resembles a trombone's, is a masterpiece of metalworking from the Late Bronze Age. Found deposited in pairs as votive offerings in northern European bogs from Scandinavia to Ireland, lurs also appear in rock carvings that show them being played in rituals.

On February 24, 1921, a Danish landowner intent on leveling a large mound of earth on his farm at Egtved in south Jutland came upon something that made him stop work immediately. The find was not at first sight spectacular; it was a tree trunk, blackened with age, that on close examination turned out to have been cut in two lengthwise. But the farmer at once suspected that he had stumbled across an ancient burial; over the previous century, similar discoveries had been made at a number of such mounds, called tumuli, scattered along the peninsula. He contacted the Danish National Museum, and an archaeologist was dispatched to investigate.

As the farmer had thought, the tree trunk was indeed a coffin. Inside, under a woolen blanket, lay the body of a blond young woman whom dental examination subsequently showed to have been between the ages of 18 and 20 at the time of her death. The body was in an extraordinarily good state of preservation; even the carefully trimmed fingernails had survived.

The clothing came as even more of a surprise *(pages 124-125)*. It had remained almost intact, revealing that the girl had been wearing a short, corded-wool skirt ending well above her knees, together with a woolen tunic with elbow-length sleeves in a style that would not look out of place in a Scandinavian boutique even today. Yet the

121

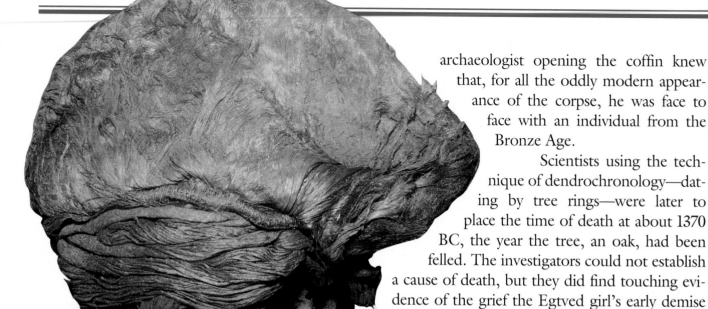

archaeologist opening the coffin knew that, for all the oddly modern appearance of the corpse, he was face to face with an individual from the Bronze Age.

Scientists using the technique of dendrochronology—dating by tree rings—were later to place the time of death at about 1370 BC, the year the tree, an oak, had been felled. The investigators could not establish a cause of death, but they did find touching evidence of the grief the Egtved girl's early demise had caused those close to her. A mourner had placed a sprig of flowering yarrow in the coffin, perhaps as a token of remembrance, a gesture disclosing that she must have died in the summertime, when the plant is in bloom.

Blond hair piled high in an elaborate headdress and looped through large gold earrings adorns the head of a young woman, about 18 years old. Dying around 1350 BC, she lay well preserved in an oak coffin found in 1935 in Skrydstrup, Denmark. Archaeologists determined that she was buried in summer; they could tell this after finding a layer of fresh grass and a delicately scented herb known as wood chervil under the animal hide on the bottom of her coffin.

The young woman had died, as it turned out, on the threshold of a time of change. For as the Bronze Age developed and matured, it was approaching its greatest crisis. By the beginning of the 12th century BC the Mediterranean civilizations of Mycenaean Greece and of Hittite Anatolia were to be wiped out, and chaos was to descend on the lands of the Levant. Change was to come to northern and western Europe too, though in less catastrophic forms.

The Late Bronze Age, as this final phase of the era is known, was to last for four or five centuries before giving way to the succeeding Iron Age in approximately 800 BC. It was a time of increasing wealth, when the benefits of the metalworker's craft spread to an ever-larger section of the population, and widening trade links bound Europe in a web of commercial connections. But it was also a period of deep insecurity, marked by the building of fortified settlements across much of the Continent. The hill fort, its houses sheltering behind palisades bristling with spiked poles, was as much a symbol of the time as were the magnificently decorated swords and shields that win the admiration of museumgoers to this day.

Few of these developments would have meant much to the Egtved girl or her family, however. For despite the trading networks that crisscrossed Europe, the inhabitants of individual communities remained largely oblivious of the wider stage around them. The Continent continued to be a patchwork of small tribes and kinship groups, even if much of their material culture was now shared across intercommunal boundaries. And the principal source of information on that culture remains the burials, which like time capsules provide intimate glimpses at the articles deemed necessary to accompany the dead to their final rest.

Some puzzling fragments of the Egtved girl's world were found buried with her, contained in two birch-bark boxes. One box held personal effects, including bronze pins, a hair ribbon, a length of knotted woolen cord of uncertain purpose, and a bronze awl; the other, on scientific examination, turned out to have contained a drink made of fermented cranberries and wheat to which honey had been added. More surprisingly still, the coffin also enclosed the cremated bones of an eight- or nine-year-old child, believed to be a girl. As the small age gap makes it unlikely that the child was the young woman's daughter, it has been suggested that she may have been a servant, sacrificed on her mistress's death to attend her in the next world.

The Egtved grave was far from unique. The practice of burying people under large tumuli had first developed in the Late Stone Age, almost 2,000 years before. By the Middle Bronze Age, burial mounds of the type in which the woman was found had been raised all over Europe, from the Balkans to the Baltic; more than 300 survive in Denmark alone, where they still form an unmistakable part of the landscape, often set on high ground commanding wide views out to sea. Many tumuli, however, had already been plundered by treasure seekers or leveled by farmers before Europe's archaeologists began to take an interest in them early in the 19th century.

When archaeologists studied the mounds, it was partly as a result of royal patronage. King Frederick VII of Denmark had a lively interest in his country's past, and he

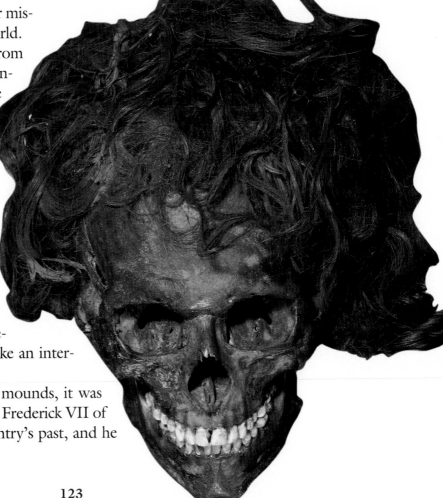

The skull of a 20-year-old youth still has a full head of hair attached. Found in one of the largest Bronze Age burial mounds in Denmark, he reclined on his back in an oak coffin with a cowhide underneath him and a wool cloak over him. His left hand held an ornamented wooden scabbard containing a six-inch-long bronze dagger. By examining the coffin, scientists could determine the precise year he was buried—1345 BC. They did so by measuring the wood's growth rings and comparing them with other ancient samples.

123

DRESSING WELL IN THE BRONZE AGE

In the decades following the discovery of three Bronze Age oak coffins at Borum Eshoj in Denmark, Europeans believed they knew how the typical female of the period dressed. Basing their judgment on the clothes of a woman in one of them, they pictured her in a concealing tunic and a full-length skirt, her hair caught up in a dowdy net with strings tied under the chin *(opposite page, far right, below)*.

So when the Egtved girl was discovered in 1921 in the coffin opposite, at upper right, the clothing she wore caused a sensation. Her short tunic left her midriff bare, and her skirt, just 16 inches long, ended above the knee. Consisting of loose strands of corded wool that were knotted at the top and bottom but otherwise swung free, the costume was far from concealing—unlike the men's wraps below and at right, also from Denmark. Some commentators refused to call it a skirt; instead, one suggested that it might have served as "an indoor garment for use in an overheated winter hut."

Three millennia after the burial of a man between the ages of 50 and 60, his woolen cape and loincloth (left) *were unearthed with his skeleton in 1875 at Borum Eshoj. Excavators found a 2½-inch-long wooden pin stuck in the side of the cape and a round woolen cap on the man's skull.*

Archaeologists digging at Muldbjerg in west Jutland in 1883 recovered leather straps and a pair of bronze fibulae along with the apparel shown above. The bands went over the shoulders, holding in place the 37-inch-long inner coat; the pins, found still attached to the collar, fastened the cape. The round woolen hat was fashioned from layers of material and is covered with thousands of knotted threads, which give it the look of fur.

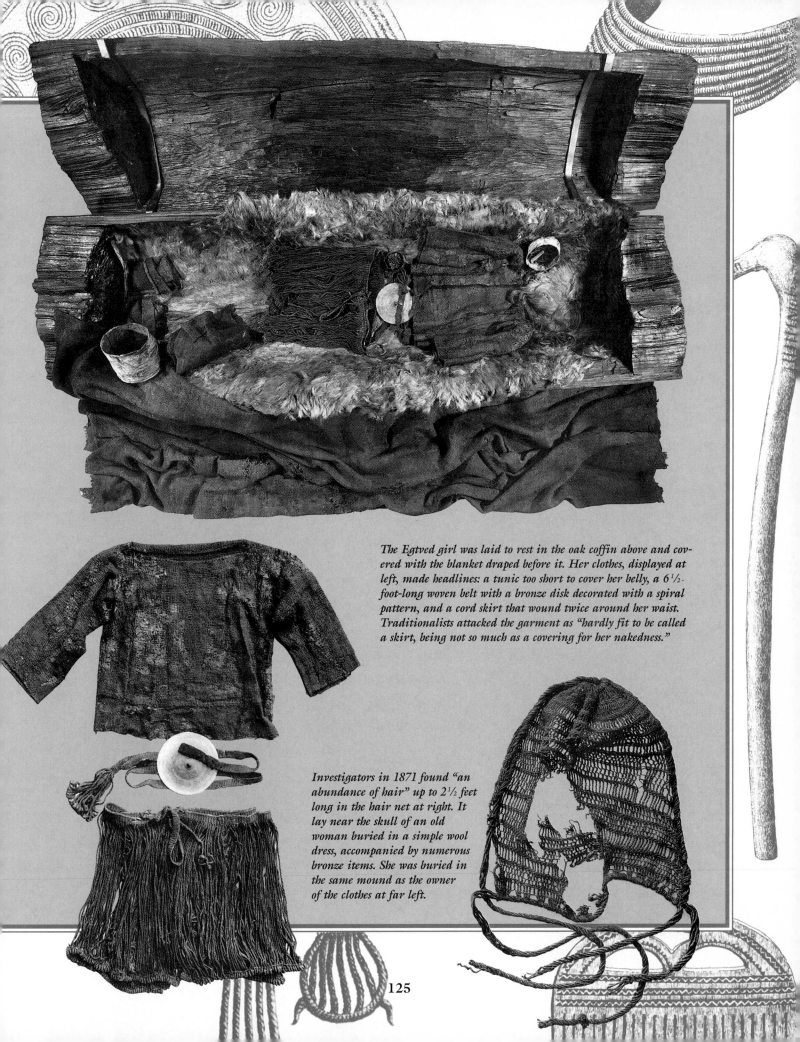

The Egtved girl was laid to rest in the oak coffin above and covered with the blanket draped before it. Her clothes, displayed at left, made headlines: a tunic too short to cover her belly, a 6½-foot-long woven belt with a bronze disk decorated with a spiral pattern, and a cord skirt that wound twice around her waist. Traditionalists attacked the garment as "hardly fit to be called a skirt, being not so much as a covering for her nakedness."

Investigators in 1871 found "an abundance of hair" up to 2½ feet long in the hair net at right. It lay near the skull of an old woman buried in a simple wool dress, accompanied by numerous bronze items. She was buried in the same mound as the owner of the clothes at far left.

personally financed the exploration of one such site at Trindhoj in 1861. He was rewarded by the discovery of a grave whose occupant's costume was still perfectly preserved, even though the wearer's bones had dissolved to a blue powder. Buried with the man were a sword and a razor, both made of bronze, and a 24-toothed comb of horn.

Other interesting finds were to turn up in other mounds. In one, investigators uncovered a 30-inch-long hazel stick that had been notched at regular intervals—perhaps a measuring rod, used in building the coffin and left behind once the job was done. Another discarded tool had had a less constructive use. This was a hooked stick found beside a coffin with a hole cut in the top. It had belonged to a Bronze Age graverobber who had sawed his way into the casket from above and then used the stick to fish out the contents, later abandoning it beside the victim whose grave he had despoiled.

Perishable materials like wood and textiles survived in the mounds by chance, through a fortuitous set of biochemical coincidences. The mounds' turf and topsoil were porous, while the hard

A leaping dancer or acrobat is one of several cast-bronze figurines dating from the eighth century BC discovered in Denmark. The young woman is dressed in ceremonial attire: a short string skirt and a neck torque. Several such figurines may have been arranged as a group in a ritual tableau, underscoring some mythical story or event.

subsoil beneath was not. In addition, the turf had a high iron content, which caused a layer of hardpan to form at the base of the mound, further strengthening the seal. As a result, the tumuli became as saturated with water as damp sponges, protecting their contents from oxygen in the same way that peat bogs sometimes do. Meanwhile, tannic acid from the oak coffins literally tanned some of the bodies, toughening the skin and also helping to combat decay.

Only in a tiny minority of cases, however, did the combination of circumstances permit the fine state of preservation of the Egtved girl. One such occurred at Skrydstrup a few miles to the south of Egtved, where in 1935 the remains of another young woman *(page 122)* of about 18 were found in a mound 40 feet in diameter. She too had had blond hair, worn piled up and held in place with a band and a hair net, but unlike her compatriot from Egtved, she was wearing an ankle-length skirt below her woolen bodice. She had elegant spirals of gold in her ears and leather moccasins on her feet.

At 5 foot 7, she was tall for her time, but not abnormally so. Examination of skeletal remains from other mounds gives an average height for the male occupants of 5 foot 8 and of 5 foot 4 for the women—less than today's 5 foot 11 and 5 foot 6, but comparing favorably with the figures of just 150 years ago, when Danish men averaged only 5 foot 5 and women barely 5 feet tall. The individuals buried in the mounds cannot, of course, be considered representative of the Bronze Age population as a whole, for as members of the wealthiest class, they were presumably better nourished and hence taller than the great majority of their contemporaries.

Prehistorians assume, in view of the amount of labor that went into the construction of the mounds, that such tombs were put up only for chieftains and their immediate families. On the average, the tumuli were about 60 feet across and 10 or more feet high, though exceptional examples could be more than twice that size. Turf from an estimated 2½ to 4 acres of pastureland was required to build them. The soil on which the mound was to be built was first plowed—traces of the furrows have been discovered—perhaps as a symbolic gesture to prepare it to receive the dead. Slabs of the turf were then built up in layers, sometimes supported by rings of stones, which served to buttress the foundations.

Surviving remnants of these settlements suggest that the so-

A kneeling female figurine of bronze from Denmark has inset gold eyes and a curled right hand that once held an object. It was discovered with a bronze, crested serpent and two long-horned animals. Bronze castings of humans, animals, and divinities began to appear in northern Europe in the eighth century BC.

called Mound people inhabited large wooden structures up to 120 feet long, the thatched roofs supported by sturdy wooden posts, with one end of the building reserved for storage or animals. The houses normally faced south to catch the most sunlight. A typical community probably housed a single extended family, though there are indications that by the latter part of the Bronze Age, villages in which several families lived together were also making their appearance.

The farm would probably have been surrounded by fields of barley, cultivated with the aid of wood plows called ards; wheat and millet might also have been grown. Stock raising was crucially important, with oxen providing most of the meat, though sheep, pigs, and horses were also eaten. If the farm was close to the coast—and nowhere in Denmark is very far away—seafood would also have figured prominently in the diet. Evidence from seasonal fishing camps indicates that cod, haddock, and flounder made up most of the catch, with shellfish as a significant addition.

Environmental studies have shown that the landscape around the farm would most likely have been an open, pastoral one, for most of northern Europe's primeval forest had by this time yielded to ax-wielding farmers. Indeed, overgrazing was becoming a problem, reducing areas of poor, sandy soil to barren heath. Yet there was probably still some woodland nearby where the farm's pigs could have rooted for acorns and the cattle grazed. These belts of uncleared forest served as boundaries, separating homesteads from their neighbors.

For details of the Mound people's possessions, nearly all the evidence consists of the grave goods buried with them. These show that the ruling

class at least had considerable wealth. Of a total of some 2,500 artifacts recovered from the mounds, about one-fifth were gold, and many of the rest consisted of finely worked bronze. Imposing swords, daggers, and axes are all commonly found, along with more domestic objects, such as razors, brooches, and pins, many of them made to a standard of craftsmanship that equaled or outdid the work of bronzesmiths anywhere else in Europe at the time.

The opulence of the finds has led prehistorians to see the period as a Nordic golden age. This sudden flowering was unexpected, because bronze had arrived late in Scandinavia: The earliest evidence of local handling of the metal dates from well into the second millennium BC, and by then the rest of Europe had used it for centuries. The first local pieces were little more than crude imitations of work from elsewhere on the Continent. But from about 1700 BC onward, bronze was being worked in large quantities, and Danish and Swedish smiths were soon rivaling and surpassing their colleagues farther south in the quality and range of the goods they produced.

Much of what is known about Nordic metalworking comes from so-called founders' hoards—deposits of scrap metal and tools buried by metal founders, or smiths, who for one reason or another were unable ever to reclaim them. Many consist of broken objects evidently destined for recycling. Others contain hammers, chisels, awls, knives, anvils, crucibles of clay and stone, half-finished castings and molds of every kind. Hundreds of such caches have been discovered, not just in Scandinavia but elsewhere in Europe. Often, the weight of the material buried corresponds to the amount one person could carry, suggesting that the hoards contained the possessions of individual smiths who sometimes transported their wares themselves.

The practice of burying valuables for safekeeping was common before door locks or strongboxes came into being, and founders' hoards are by no means the only such finds known to archaeologists. Collections of tools and weapons in mint condition are also sometimes discovered; these are usually categorized as merchants' hoards, on the assumption that they were trade goods that never found a purchaser. Other finds in which ornaments, tools, and weapons are mixed together may have been personal repositories, secreted by their owners in times of trouble and never reclaimed. Hoards of all types became more common as the Bronze Age pro-

These hammered gold bowls dating from 1000 to 800 BC may have been used as ritual vessels and then sacrificed in a Danish bog. Although they were probably imported from central Europe, the one at the bottom displays a northern touch: A handle in the form of a little horsehead was added locally.

gressed; they declined in number only from about 500 BC on, by which time bronze had largely been replaced by iron.

The sudden upsurge in bronze production is the more surprising in that Scandinavia had no local supplies of either copper or tin, the metals needed to make the alloy. All of the smith's raw materials had to be imported over great distances. One possible source was Britain; but by far the greater part seems to have come from the mines of central Europe, some brought via trade routes stretching up the Elbe River. Denmark, which lay closest to the sources of supply, quickly became the center of the new industry, but southern Sweden and Norway also participated actively. Only in northern Scandinavia did bronze objects remain rare; there, a separate hunting culture retained an older way of life, and the relatively few bronze objects that have been found apparently came in through barter, or exchange.

By the latter part of the Bronze Age, the appetite for the metal in the Nordic lands had become considerable. One researcher, working from the evidence provided by archaeological finds in Denmark alone, has estimated that up to one-quarter of a ton of bronze would have been needed annually simply to make up for the amount buried in graves or hoards. By extrapolation, that would suggest a total stock in circulation of from 5 to $7\frac{1}{2}$ tons.

Prehistorians have long puzzled over the question of what the Nordic lands supplied in return for the copper and tin imports on which their smiths depended. The most obvious commodity they had to offer in exchange was amber. This mysterious and beautiful fossilized resin was prized for its decorative qualities and reputed to have magical healing powers. It was found in several parts of Europe, but by far the most plentiful supply came from the Baltic, where pieces from undersea deposits were regularly washed up on the beaches after storms. Archaeological discoveries suggest that its use was largely restricted to the Baltic region until the third millennium BC, but from that time on its distribution expanded over much of Europe; amber ornaments turn up in graves as far apart as southern England and Poland. Objects decorated with amber shown by spectroscopic analysis to have come from the Baltic have even been found in graves dated to 1600 BC at Mycenae in Greece .

Usually, tombs containing amber artifacts are also rich in other valuables, suggesting that the material was highly prized. Yet at approximately the same time that amber started cropping up in burials around continental Europe, it all but disappeared from Baltic graves.

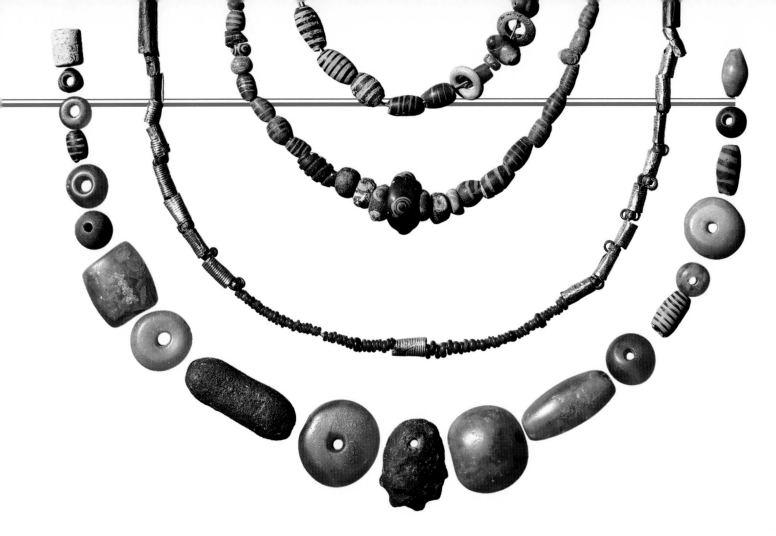

Strings of beads made of amber, colored glass, and gold—all probably acquired through trade—were recovered at settlement sites in Switzerland. Amber is one indication of the magnitude of commerce during northern Europe's Bronze Age; amber has been found in rich burials from south Britain to central Germany, far from its Baltic source.

It seems that from that time forward the resin was primarily reserved for trade. Evidence of the trade turned up in the shape of a 6½-pound lump of amber found buried in a Bronze Age clay vessel on the shore of northern Jutland; it would presumably have been exchanged for copper and tin or for luxury goods that were unobtainable locally.

Other goods no doubt also found their way down the trade routes to the south. For example, there was probably a demand for Scandinavian furs, because the pelts of northern foxes, seals, martens, and bears were heavier and thicker than the skins available in warmer climes. Yet because of their perishable nature they have left no trace in the archaeological record.

One researcher has suggested that the Scandinavians may have exported their womenfolk, and that the bride price paid for them may have brought further wealth to the northern lands. The evidence for this notion lies in the fact that necklaces, bracelets, and other Nordic female ornaments are found in hoards and burials much farther to the south than are male objects, such as swords and axes. In addition, burials of a Scandinavian type are more common in northern Germany than north European graves are in Scandinavia. The implication is that Danish and Swedish women may frequently have married husbands to the south, smoothing the way for trading connections as well as boosting their families' possessions through their bride prices.

However the people of Scandinavian lands obtained the copper and tin for their bronze, they certainly made good use of it once they had it. Northern metalsmiths excelled at the use of sheet metalworking and multiple-piece molds, and also helped develop tougher swords, with the hilt and blade cast in a single piece. Among their most spectacular creations were the curving horns known as lurs *(page 120)*. About 35 of these ceremonial instruments, typically four feet long, have been found in graves and hoards in Denmark, and smaller numbers have also turned up in Norway, Sweden, Ireland, and northern Germany. The shape of the lurs seems to have been inspired by the horns of oxen, and they are usually found buried in pairs, again suggesting a parallel with animal horns. They were cast in individual sections joined with rings, permitting them to be dismantled for carrying. Twentieth-century musicians who have experimented with them have found that they produce a distinctive, mournful sound and have a wide tonal range, similar to that of the modern trombone.

Representations of lurs in rock carvings suggest that they were used in sacred ceremonies, but investigators can only guess what form those rituals may have taken. In the absence of written texts, the nature of Bronze Age religion, in Scandinavia as elsewhere in Europe, remains a mystery that is made more intriguing by the enigmatic glimpses of ritual practice that archaeology occasionally finds.

What, for instance, was the significance of the many valuable bronze objects found discarded, apparently deliberately, in rivers and swamps across Scandinavia and other parts of northern Europe, a practice that would continue well into the Iron Age. Swords were the articles most commonly jettisoned in this way, bringing to mind images of King Arthur and his magical sword Excalibur, which had to be thrown into a lake before the monarch could die in peace. However, other objects, including helmets, tools, and on occasion even complete sets of women's ornaments, were also sometimes forfeited. Most commentators see in these so-called votive hoards propitiatory offerings designed to win the favor of the gods, or else perhaps to avert their jealousy by sharing wealth with them.

The sun played a central role in northern religious belief, or so it would seem from the single most outstanding ritual artifact to

This bronze hoard, uncovered by a peat cutter in Poland and dated at 1000 BC, included, among other objects, a spear head, sword handle, several gorgets, or ornamental collars, and a range of brooches, some with spiral appendages. The designs of the brooches may have proclaimed the wearer's special status.

have survived from the Scandinavian Bronze Age. This is a remarkable solar chariot, found in pieces by a farmer plowing previously uncultivated bogland at Trundholm in northern Zealand in 1902. Not realizing its significance, the man gave it to his daughter to play with as a toy until word of the find reached the Danish National Museum and experts arrived at the farm to claim the object for the nation.

The Trundholm Chariot consists of a horse pulling a vehicle holding a bronze disk sheathed on one side in a paper-thin covering of gold; both horse and chariot are set on wheels, perhaps to allow the image to be drawn in procession. The idea of the sun traveling across the heavens in a chariot is a familiar one in several religions: In classical mythology, for example, Apollo was its driver. Evidence that some similar concept existed in Bronze Age Europe comes not just from this one piece but also from large circles of bronze—perhaps sun disks—that have been found in a number of graves. Indeed, fragments of another sun chariot were found at Helsingborg in 1895, but in such a damaged state that they were thrown away.

To judge from the amount of effort put into the building of tombs, death and burial must have occupied a central part in the belief system of the Bronze Age, in Scandinavia as well as in other parts of Europe. Yet what little is known about the funeral rites themselves comes mainly from eight stone slabs forming the sides of a tomb that were discovered at a rock cairn site at Kivik in southern Sweden in 1748 *(pages 136-137)*. The slabs show axes, horses, ships, and sun wheels, arranged symmetrically in pairs. Other images apparently illustrate the ceremonies themselves: There are people in robes in procession, a man driving a wagon, a charioteer, musicians beating drums and blowing lurs. Human sacrifice is even suggested by depictions of three men apparently with no arms—perhaps they are tied behind their backs—being confronted by a fourth with a drawn sword. Significantly, lurs have been found interred alongside animal and human bones that may be mementos of just such grim practices.

Similar images to those found at Kivik are also repeated in the paintings and carvings that decorate large, flat rock surfaces at many sites in Scandinavia, and particularly in southern Sweden. Dating such images is difficult, but the weapons and tools depicted in them are mostly those of the Late Bronze Age. The objects most commonly shown, even at inland sites, are ships, and these representa-

The nearly two-foot-long Trundholm Chariot consists of a hollow cast-bronze horse drawing a sun disk covered on one face with gold, all set on a base of three pairs of bronze wheels. Discovered by a Danish farmer plowing a new field, this unique object, thought to emphasize the important role of the sun in religious beliefs of Bronze Age peoples, may have been wheeled across a ceremonial stage in a ritual re-enactment of the sun's daily journey across the heavens. The gilded side of the disk may very well have represented day, and the opposite, bronze side, night.

tions are the best surviving indications of what early Scandinavian boats looked like. They are shown with peaked prows and sterns, resembling later Viking vessels, and often have a pole that extends forward below the water line, presumably serving as a battering ram. Sometimes the ships carry as many as 40 oarsmen, rowing in pairs.

Oxen, horses, plows, and deer also feature repeatedly in the carvings, as do wheeled disks, which are usually interpreted as solar symbols, and hollowed-out cup marks, typically about two inches across, whose purpose is unknown. Human figures are less common, but where they do appear they are normally males with exaggerated sexual characteristics. Sometimes these extraordinarily virile figures are shown plowing; in at least one case, a man is mating with a cow. All in all, the theme of fertility is hard to miss.

Equally intriguing are a few scenes depicting what look like ritual activities, often involving men carrying lurs, axes, or less frequently, bows. Presumably they illustrate Bronze Age cults, but the present state of knowledge is insufficient to explain what is going on.

One extraordinary carving from the Swedish province of Skane shows a horned, gesticulating figure wearing an animal skin complete with antler. The image is bizarre enough to instantly bring to mind the supernatural, and the man is generally taken to be some kind of sorcerer or shaman, perhaps in the act of transformation. As it happens, burial sites have provided independent signs suggesting that witchcraft of some sort may have been practiced in Bronze Age Scandinavia. These signs take the form of

leather bags containing selections of objects that would not be out of place in the witches' incantations in Shakespeare's *Macbeth*—including in one case a falcon's claw, the lower jaw of a squirrel, a snake's tail, dried roots, a flint knife, and a small pair of tweezers.

Many of the motifs of the Scandinavian paintings and carvings, including sorcerer figures, reappear in another cluster of rock art 700 miles to the south in Val Camonica in the Italian Alps. Sun disks, oxen, stags, and cup-and-ring markings all feature prominently among these carvings, which have been thoroughly studied and documented by the Italian scholar Emmanuel Anati *(page 92)*. An even more unexpected gallery of carvings lies 200 miles to the southwest, between 6,000 and 9,000 feet up on the slopes of Monte Bego on the Franco-Italian border. Here, in a cluster of remote and barren mountain valleys, images of oxen decorate the glacially scoured rock faces, alongside depictions of plows, human figures, daggers, swords, and serpents. In all, this wasteland shelters as many as 100,000 carvings on some 40,000 different rock surfaces.

A drawing published in the 1780s of the entrance to the Kivik grave in Sweden illustrates one of the engraved slabs that once lined its interior; this slab has since been lost. The axes have helped date the site to approximately 1000 BC.

If Scandinavian Bronze Age rock art has parallels elsewhere in Europe, so too do the votive hoards. Investigating the flat, waterlogged fenland of eastern England in 1982, archaeologist Francis Pryor came across evidence at Flag Fen of thousands of ancient wooden posts underlying what is now drained farmland. Through careful reconstruction he was able to determine that the posts had formed a platform, set in what was then a marshy inlet of an inland waterway. Two causeways linked this artificial island to dry land. One estimate suggests that the whole complex may have required the wood of as many as four million trees.

At first Pryor assumed that he had uncovered a settlement built upon the water for defensive purposes. But a later find led him to revise that opinion. Some 300 metal objects, ranging from valuable bronze swords to ornaments such as rings and pins, were found scattered near the island, apparently thrown into what had been open water around the causeways. Even more unexpectedly, many of the artifacts had been deliberately damaged before they were jettisoned; with a single exception, all the swords had been bent or snapped in half, while an ax had had its haft laboriously snapped in two. The way the broken parts were grouped indicated that the objects had been dropped intentionally into the water, probably from boats.

The finds led Pryor to the conclusion that he was dealing with some type of religious monument where, for reasons that can still only be guessed at, votive offerings were made on a massive scale. "Perhaps the waters of Flag Fen brought special good fortune in love, in the hunt, or in any other important aspect of life," he has written. "Some of the items must have been dropped into the waters with cheering crowds and much rejoicing; others might have marked the end of a long and distinguished life; still others were doubtless private acts of longing, regret, or recrimination. All of human life is there, had we the power to see it."

Various goods moved as freely as religious concepts and rituals throughout Europe toward the end of the Bronze Age. As a matter of fact, one of the characteristics of the time was a remarkably homogeneous material culture, and similar styles of metalwork and

Scenes on two of the eight slabs from the Kivik grave may depict the solemn interment of the dead. The stylized carving on the seventh slab (below, left) *seems to show a two-wheeled chariot with horse and driver, four men carrying swords, a middle row of sacrificial animals, and at the bottom, a funeral procession of mourners. The eighth slab* (below, right) *shows men playing lurs and striking a drum, a row of mourners around a sacred cauldron, and at the bottom, a burial ceremony occurring outside omega-shaped tombs.*

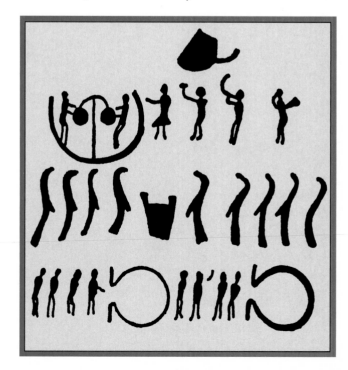

pottery turn up from Czechoslovakian lands to the English Channel.

The size of the various hoards from this period suggests that there was more bronze in circulation than ever before. Metal tools such as sickles and axes were more freely available, leading to improvements in agricultural efficiency. Also at hand was an abundance of bronze swords, daggers, rapiers, and metal-tipped spears. The Bronze Age had seen a revolution in the technology of combat; weapons had become more lethal, and perhaps for the first time, they were being designed specifically to kill humans rather than animals. With their diffusion, a new fear spread of armed raiders—the ruthless men who would all too willingly put their lethal arsenals to use.

In this nervous, newly wealthy Europe, in which for the first time elite groups had considerable stores of personal possessions, trading and exchange connections assumed increasing importance. The very nature of bronze encouraged such developments by requiring supplies of tin and copper to be brought together for alloying. But other commodities were also in demand. Alongside finished bronze products, gold, faience beads, and even seashells were all actively traded. So was graphite, used to add a metalic sheen to fine pottery; in central Europe one-third of all the ceramics found in Late Bronze Age graves were adorned with this foreign element.

The greater part of the traffic was probably carried out locally, through interlocking circles of regional exchange networks. A once-popular concept of itinerant merchants crisscrossing the Con-

A horned and phallic figure ceremoniously leaps above the crew of a Bronze Age ship, engraved among numerous other rock carvings in Bohuslan, Sweden. Aboard the vessel various rites and celebrations seem to be taking place. The raising of one or both arms overhead, for example, has been interpreted by scholars as an attitude of worhip. Motifs such as ships, disks, footprints, and various weapons are often represented in Scandinavian rock art of the period.

Harnessed to a yoke and driven by a phallic stick figure holding a tree branch, oxen break ground drawing a Bronze Age ard, a plow formed by a forked tree branch. Like other Swedish rock carvings of the period, this one seems to depict a fertility rite, vital to the agricultural life of Bronze Age Europeans.

tinent to supply the precious commodities now finds few supporters. Instead, prehistorians prefer to imagine a system of local elites carrying out exchanges with their neighboring counterparts and then redistributing the acquired goods within their own territory through gift giving, bride buying, and other customary practices. No doubt many valuables also passed from group to group as spoils of war. Whatever the means, objects certainly moved over considerable distances, as they had already done for thousands of years past; only now they traveled in greater quantities than ever.

By far the major part of this long-distance trade was in the luxury items that elite groups would have wished to own, whether to proclaim their own status or to trade with similarly privileged neighbors. But one commodity at least was a necessity that whole communities needed to survive. This was salt, widely used to preserve meat and fish. So important was it that the salt-mining center of Hallstatt in what is now Austria was to give its name to a whole culture of the ensuing Iron Age; and exploitation of the mineral was already well-established there before the Bronze Age ended. Other important centers grew up near salt pans in southern Poland and eastern Germany, and many coastal regions must also have prospered from

139

trading in sea salt. Certainly evidence from Walton-on-the-Naze, on the east coast of England, indicates that seawater was being trapped in large troughs and boiled down to salt crystals as early as 1100 BC.

Many of the goods that moved from community to community no doubt still traveled on people's backs, as they had done since the days of the New Stone Age. But there is evidence that horses were increasingly being used as draft animals. Bits and harness items start to appear in graves over much of eastern Europe as early as 2000 BC, but the frequency of such finds increases greatly as the Bronze Age wears on. Indeed, of 24 representations of wheeled vehicles in Scandinavian rock carvings from the later Bronze Age, 22 are pulled by horses; only two show oxcarts, which would previously have been the norm. To accommodate the increased traffic, new, long-distance thoroughfares came into existence; the Ridgeway along the summit of the Wiltshire and Berkshire Downs, often called England's oldest road, probably dates from this time.

Evidence from shipwrecks suggests that seaborne transport may also have played a part in the burgeoning commerce of the day. A vessel found on the seabed off the coast of southern Turkey in 1958 turned out to be carrying a bronze merchant's entire stock in trade, including metal ingots, tools—including axes, chisels, and punches—and a portable workshop for producing goods to order, complete with a forge, hammers, anvils, and crucibles. In all, almost one ton of metal was recovered.

No such complete find has come from farther west, although a metal hoard discovered in a river estuary in Spain, and thought to have come from a sunken ship, contained swords of a type found along the Atlantic coast as far north as Britain; also included were other weapons and ornaments from a wide range of locations. Similar finds off southern England were made up of metal artifacts of French types that were probably being shipped across the English Channel for import into Britain. If these interpretations are correct, large quantities of metal were undoubtedly moved by sea.

For evidence of the social consequences of the increase in trade, researchers again turn to the burial sites and the evidence of personal wealth that they contain. As it happens, a major change in the treatment of the dead affected all Europe in the years after 1500 BC. Perhaps starting in eastern Europe and then spreading quite rapidly across the rest of the Continent, cremation—previously a relatively rare practice—now became the norm. By the mid-13th centu-

Smoke rises from thatch-roofed houses of a Bronze Age settlement, depicted here in a reconstruction of a site at Mucking, on the Thames River, in England. A screen of large timbers in the center divides the domestic area from a ceremonial, ritual area in front. This type of circular enclosure—which became common in Europe during the Bronze Age, when tribes began raiding one another—is protected by a deep ditch, earthen ramparts, and a tower at the narrow causeway entrance.

ry, most Europeans were cremated on their death and buried in urns in large cemeteries.

Certain styles of bronzework, pottery, and even house building accompanied the new funerary customs, leading prehistorians in the past to postulate that a people of unknown origin spread across the Continent at this time, bringing the new ways with them. Because Celtic populations were known to have been in place in western Europe by the ensuing Iron Age, these supposed migrants were sometimes referred to as proto-Celts, ancestors of the Gauls, ancient Britons, and other peoples familiar from the accounts of the classical historians. The newcomers are also known as Urnfield people, for their practice of burying the ashes of their dead in cremation urns.

Further investigation has shown, however, that there was also

much that did not change in western societies at the time, undermining the notion of an entirely new social order. It now seems that if proto-Celts did indeed arrive in Europe in the last centuries of the second millennium, they must have done so for the most part peacefully rather than as a destructive invading force. For want of conclusive evidence, most scholars have begun questioning the existence of an Urnfield people sweeping over Europe from the east. Still, they accept the reality of the cultural changes associated with this people, and are generally happy to refer to the latter part of the Bronze Age as the Urnfield Culture.

Status possessions continued to be buried in the Urnfield period, frequently in or next to the cremation urns. Unsurprisingly, the richest cemeteries tend to be those nearest to the sources of sought-after raw materials; graves in the middle and upper Danube region, not far from abundant sources of copper and tin, were particularly well provided. Within the burial grounds, there is a marked division between rich and poor graves, as there had been in earlier times. Typically, about one grave in 100 includes status items such as swords, belts decorated with gold or bronze, or finely made vessels. Others will have less prestigious items such as razors, knives, and ornaments of lesser value, but the majority run only to pots and perhaps a single ornament. A fourth category holds nothing but cremated bones.

Taken as a whole, the evidence of the cemeteries suggests that, while Europe became richer in metalware and other status goods, the benefits were far from evenly shared. If anything, the new wealth served rather to polarize social divisions within communities. With new wealth, society effectively became more divided.

An extreme example of individual magnificence comes from one exceptional burial site found by archaeologist Josef Paulik in 1953 at Ockov, a village in western Slovakia. Excavation revealed that the body of its occupant, presumably a prominent member of the warrior elite, had been burned on a funeral pyre at least 30 feet wide; the cremated remains were then buried deep beneath the ashes of the conflagration. Molten remnants indicated that a treasure in gold ornaments, bronze weapons, and other valuables had been consumed by the flames during the cremation. After the ashes had been interred, the whole site was topped with a mound of earth 20 feet high and surrounded by a stone wall to provide a permanent memorial.

An eight-inch-long cast-bronze wagon unearthed in Bavaria, Germany, at a rich burial site dating from the 12th century BC, holds a bronze vessel of undetermined use. This and similar miniature wagons found across Europe may have been used for ritual purposes before being interred in the graves of wealthy individuals.

As he investigated the site, Paulik quickly noted striking parallels between what he was unearthing and the funerals of heroes described in the Greek poet Homer's *Iliad*. In this great epic—believed to have been composed in the eighth century BC and to have described a Late Bronze Age world—the body of the warrior Patroclus is consumed on a 100-foot pyre, under which his ashes are subsequently buried. As at the Slovakian site, the burial place is then topped by a mound and ringed by a wall. In the Homeric version, jars of honey and of oil are placed on the fire; similarly, vases that had contained liquids were found at Ockov. Finally, Achilles in burying Patroclus did what the poet described as "an evil thing" by killing a dozen Trojan prisoners and putting their bodies on the pyre. At Ockov too, vessels containing cremated human bones—possibly those of sacrificed victims—were found within the mound.

Even though the burial site of the Ockov warlord remains the only one of its kind discovered so far, it seems likely that military elites were active on a smaller scale all over Europe in the later Bronze Age, sparking the growing armory. It is easy to imagine such men encased in the bronze body armor that was an innovation of the time, no doubt cutting striking figures in their gleaming helmets, cuirass-

ARMOR OF THE WARRIOR ARISTOCRACY

Archaeologists excavating such widely separated sites as the urn-fields of central Europe and the bogs of Scandinavia and Great Britain have uncovered pieces of Late Bronze Age armor that are strikingly similar. Most are made of sheet metal too thin for combat and are thought to have been decorative—or ceremonial. Indeed, much of the armor was probably ritually buried. The helmets at right came from a Danish peat bog. One stood on a wooden tray; the other was tucked in an earthenware bowl. The headpieces tell the extent of Bronze Age trade: Although they were found on a northern island, they are believed to have been made far to the south, in Italy.

Long horns thought to be symbols of virility crown the helmets at right, discovered in 1942 on the Danish island of Zealand. Like the ribbed shield below—which was beaten into shape about 800 BC and found in 1784 in a bog in Caernarvonshire, Wales—the headgear was probably intended for display, not for combat.

The embossed cuirass above was unearthed at Marmesse, in northern
France, some 300 miles from Pergine
Valsugana, Italy, the find spot of the
greave, or shin guard, at left. Apparently, similar pieces were worn by Bronze
Age warriors all across Europe, as the
nine-inch-tall bronze figure at right
shows. Body armor encases his chest and
back, and greaves run from knees to
ankles, while a horned helmet like the
ones at far left sits atop his head. He
clutches swords and a circular shield.
The statuette was unearthed in 1841 on
the island of Sardinia.

OPENING THE GRAVES OF TIME'S PEOPLE

Archaeologists have excavated bodies in various states of preservation at a dozen sites around the Tarim Basin, an area measuring some 500 miles from east to west and 400 miles north to south. This region is bounded on three sides by mountains that block precipitation and contribute to its aridity. At one time it was the heartland of Eurasia, with a succession of oases fed by mountain streams serving as a lure to travelers and to immigrants who seem to have entered the basin first from the northwest, then the southwest, and later the east. Their routes were destined to become branches of the famed Silk Road, which flourished roughly between 130 BC and AD 1300. Today's inhabitants, descendants of people who are documented to have been in the area as early as the first century BC, are Muslim Turkic-speaking Uygurs, China's fifth-largest ethnic group, with a population of over seven million.

Although ancient bodies had been randomly coming to light in the region for years, a dedicated scientific effort did not get under way until the late 1970s, when archaeological teams made up of both Chinese and Uygurs began their investigations. Prehistoric cemeteries such as the one above, far right, near the village of Wupu (or, in Uygur, Qaradöwä) are usually located along riverbeds. Indeed, the name Wupu indicates that the spot was the fifth in a series of oases stretching out into the desert near the modern town of Hami (Qomul). In ancient times poplars lined the rivers. Logs from these trees, probably cut with bronze tools, roof the grave pits. The poplars suggest a somewhat more hospitable environment than today's, one that could have supported a pastoral, sheepherding culture.

Arms clutched to chest and knees drawn up in the fetal position, the 3,200-year-old body of a young woman of about 20—her long, reddish hair intact—was unearthed in 1979 near the village of Qaradöwä in the Xinjiang Uygur region. Her pose reflects the boxy grave space in which she lay. Poorly conserved, her skin gleams with a shellaclike substance that was applied soon after her discovery and has caused discoloration.

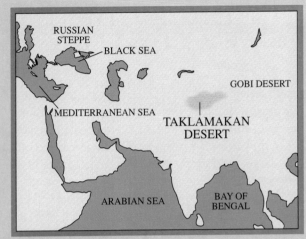

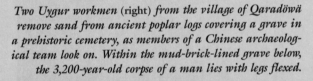

The Taklamakan Desert, southwest of the Gobi Desert, lies in the heart of central Asia and was once punctuated by oases linking Bronze Age trade routes. Some scholars think it likely early Indo-European peoples from the Russian Steppe wandered into the region and made it their home.

Two Uygur workmen (right) from the village of Qaradöwä remove sand from ancient poplar logs covering a grave in a prehistoric cemetery, as members of a Chinese archaeological team look on. Within the mud-brick-lined grave below, the 3,200-year-old corpse of a man lies with legs flexed.

TOUCHING EVIDENCE OF EVERYDAY LIFE

One of the researchers studying the origins of the ancient Caucasoid inhabitants of the Taklamakan Desert is Victor Mair, a linguist at the University of Pennsylvania. Gathering clues from the bodies themselves, the clothes they wear, and grave goods, as well as from linguistic studies and DNA research, he hopes eventually to be able to say where these people originated. Did they have a direct link to the Bronze Age cultures of Europe? Were they originally Steppe dwellers, horse-borne sheepherders driven by a nomadic way of life onto ever new frontiers?

The presence of horse remains and wheels in second-millennium graves near Qomul suggests a link to the Steppe of southern Russia, the Ukraine, and central Asia, where scientists believe the horse was domesticated and the wheel invented. By improving mobility, horse and wheel would have permitted the widespread dispersal of nomadic groups. A shred of evidence *(below)* found at Qaradöwä also points to a possible European connection. It is a piece of plaid cloth, woven around 1200 BC from blue, white, and brown wool, probably on a warp-weighted loom; significantly, the weave is a twill, common then in northern Europe but not yet seen in textiles of the same period from China.

A 13-inch-high, pointed felt hat of brown wool (above) *is reminiscent of headgear seen in Persian bas-reliefs and is much like a type of hat commonly worn by nomadic tribes in central Asia. The Scythian, or Saka, people are known in Persian histories as the Saka tigrakhanda, or "Saka, who wear pointed hats." This and 12 other hats of varying styles, dating to 1000 BC, were discovered in 1985 at Zaghunluq in Cherchen, near the southeast edge of the Taklamakan Desert, by Uygur archaeologist Dolkun Kamberi. The plaid fabric at right, from a cemetery near Qomul, was studied by University of Pennsylvania textile expert Irene Good and found to be similar to European cloth fragments dating from 1100 BC to 500 BC.*

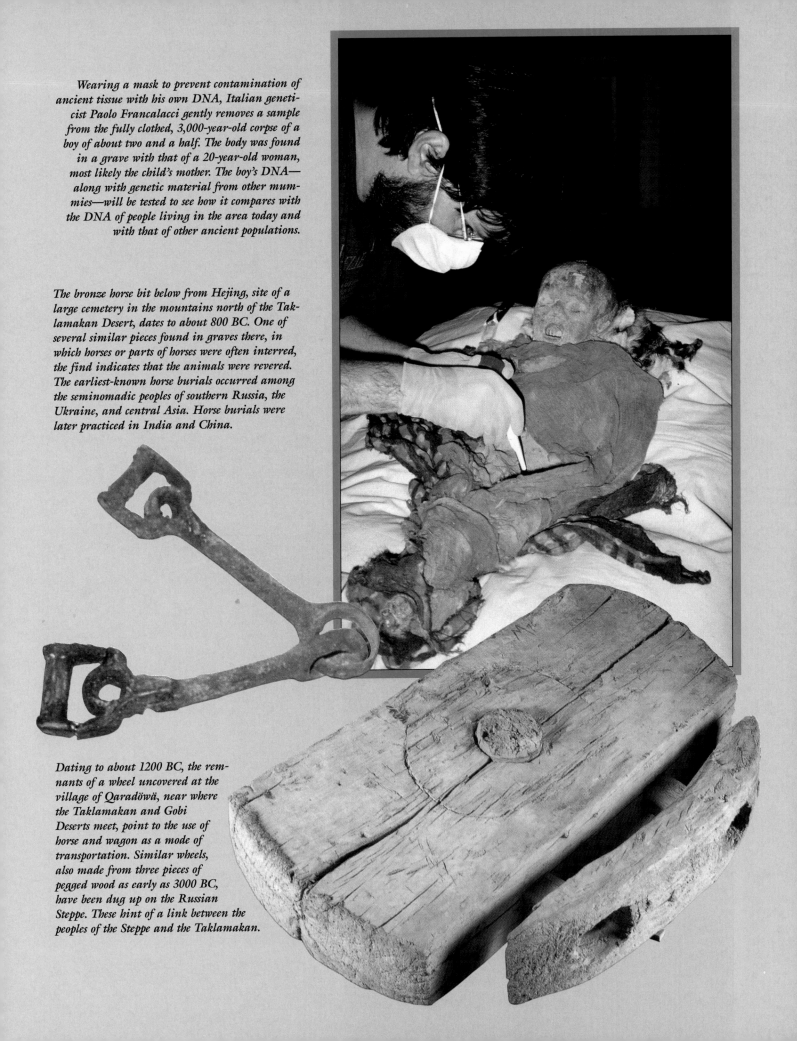

Wearing a mask to prevent contamination of ancient tissue with his own DNA, Italian geneticist Paolo Francalacci gently removes a sample from the fully clothed, 3,000-year-old corpse of a boy of about two and a half. The body was found in a grave with that of a 20-year-old woman, most likely the child's mother. The boy's DNA—along with genetic material from other mummies—will be tested to see how it compares with the DNA of people living in the area today and with that of other ancient populations.

The bronze horse bit below from Hejing, site of a large cemetery in the mountains north of the Taklamakan Desert, dates to about 800 BC. One of several similar pieces found in graves there, in which horses or parts of horses were often interred, the find indicates that the animals were revered. The earliest-known horse burials occurred among the seminomadic peoples of southern Russia, the Ukraine, and central Asia. Horse burials were later practiced in India and China.

Dating to about 1200 BC, the remnants of a wheel uncovered at the village of Qaradöwä, near where the Taklamakan and Gobi Deserts meet, point to the use of horse and wagon as a mode of transportation. Similar wheels, also made from three pieces of pegged wood as early as 3000 BC, have been dug up on the Russian Steppe. These hint of a link between the peoples of the Steppe and the Taklamakan.

FACES OF PREHISTORY BROUGHT TO LIGHT

The startling 3,000-year-old mummies shown on this and the following pages are from excavations conducted in 1985 by Uygur archaeologist Dolkun Kamberi at Cherchen, site of a vanished city on a river that wandered miles away and dried up. All of the graves studied contained reeds—either loose or woven into mats. Since reeds require moisture to grow well, they signified the presence of enough water to support grass and sheep. Enough remains of the animals turned up to suggest their owners were herders.

The area's inhabitants may well have been related to the Scythians, or Saka, whom Greek historian Herodotus refers to as living in the region. But, as Kamberi points out, "Central Asia was a very fluid place at that point in history. Remains, artifacts, bronze objects from the same ancient time frame are very similar from Western China to Hungary." The problem is compounded by the fact that while archaeology of the Steppe dwellers has been going on for some time, investigation of the Taklamakan is only now getting under way.

Members of an archaeological team lift the mummy of a man out of an eight-foot-deep grave that also contained three female corpses. The grave's lower level, where the women lay, was covered by a large brown wool robe and a white felt blanket, on which sat a leather saddle and a single black pottery jar. Willow mats covered the floor; a gutter ran around the edge to drain away moisture from the bodies. Close by, the archaeologist Dolkun Kamberi dug up the skull and foreleg of a horse. The leg bone had been removed, leaving the skin and hoof, which had been stuffed with reeds—a unique variation on traditional horse burials.

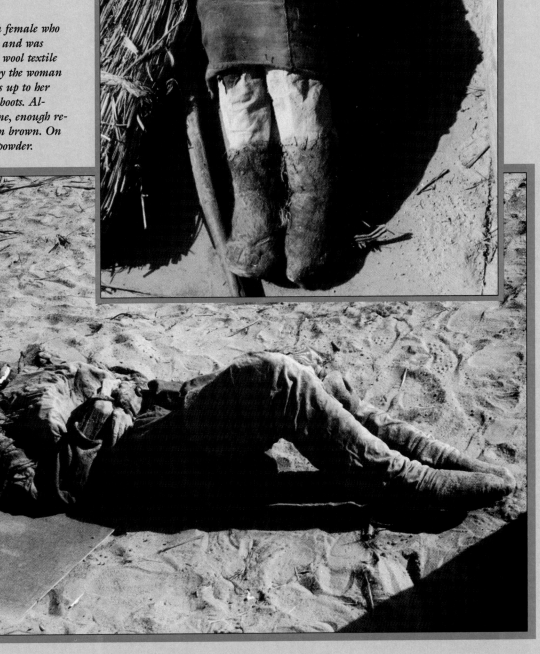

Lying beside a bundle of reeds from her grave, this fully clothed woman was buried with various everyday items, including knitting needles, a wood milking pail, combs, and pottery. She wears a calf-length, reddish brown wool dress, and socks and boots identical to those on a man's body from the same grave. Two artificial braids had been added to her already-braided yellowish brown hair.

The less well preserved body of a female who stood about five feet tall in life and was 50 years old at death wears red wool textile almost identical to that worn by the woman above. She too has red wool socks up to her thighs, and knee-high deerskin boots. Although most of her hair was gone, enough remained to show that it had been brown. On her cheeks was a trace of ocher powder.

Thanks to the salty conditions of his grave, this male—who stood about six feet tall in life—is among the most perfectly preserved of the Taklamakan mummies. He is dressed in trousers and a short jacket, both of purple wool; multicolored wool socks; and knee-high white deerskin boots. Around his wrist is a wool bracelet. The body was found lying on its side, on a layer of willow mats; it had been propped up with a stick and faced a natural salt wall.

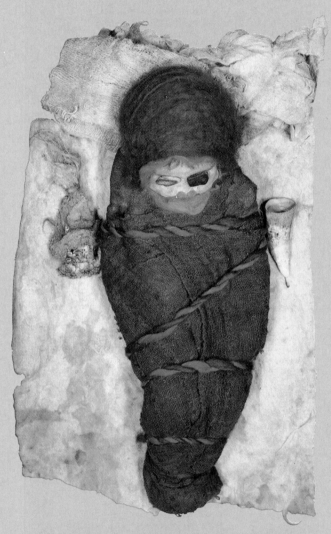

In a shallow grave lay the corpse of this infant, not yet three months old. Laid out on a white felt blanket and wool pillow, it was swaddled in purple wool, tightly bound with wool string. On the head was a blue wool hat, and small flat stones covered the eyes. Near the body Dolkun Kamberi found a small drinking horn and a baby's bottle made of a sheep's teat with milk residue inside. Next to it was a sheep's head, perhaps left as a sacrifice.

A close-up (above) of the mummy at left shows eyelashes, eyebrows, and beard intact. The yellowish brown hair, which had begun to turn white, was wound into two 12-inch-long braids. Yellow ocher applied to the forehead in a sun spiral can still be seen. The wood spoon employed was left behind in the grave, with pigment clinging to it. The custom of using ocher in burials began 30,000 to 40,000 years ago, and the practice was to become prevalent in central Asia and Europe.

A LONG JOURNEY INTO THE AGE OF IRON

ICE AGE/OLD STONE AGE
2,000,000-12,000 BC

CARVED BISON

Some two million years ago, the alternating advance and retreat of monstrous glaciers ushered in a protracted ice age, imposing cycles of warming and cooling on much of the northern hemisphere. At about the same time, in temperate Africa, an early species of humans known to modern scholars as *Homo habilis* were using the stone choppers, blades, and other such implements that, with refinements along the way, would hallmark their descendants for millennia. By about one million years later, these Old Stone Age humans had learned to use fire for such things as cooking, warmth, and keeping predators at bay; it was then that *Homo erectus,* having evolved from *Homo habilis,* began a long, slow northward spread that would, by at least 500,000 years ago, take individuals into Ice Age Europe.

Challenged by the demands of a harsher climate, the migrants developed into a species called Neanderthal. Well-adapted to the cold, Neanderthals lived in organized groups and thrived for some 120,000 years, until they were completely replaced about 30,000 years ago by fully modern humans, *Homo sapiens,* often referred to as Cro-Magnons.

The Cro-Magnons' origins are uncertain, as is the precise fate of the Neanderthals. Indeed, it was once believed that Neanderthals might simply have evolved into Cro-Magnons. Most scholars today, however, hold that *Homo sapiens* probably arose in the Middle East; from there individuals migrated to Europe, where they interbred with Neanderthals and eventually subsumed them into a new group of modern Europeans.

What is certain is that the surviving Cro-Magnons were far more advanced than the Neanderthals. They not only produced finer stone tools, but also created delicate objects of art, such as the carved bison above. Crafted from a reindeer antler some 16,000 years ago, it was the head of a spear-thrower.

MIDDLE AND NEW STONE AGES
13,000-2000 BC

GOD FIGURE WITH SICKLE

By 12,000 BC, the world's climate was warming. Living now in a relatively stable and temperate environment, early Europeans began to dwell in settled communities. Spurring the development was the introduction of agriculture, thought to have arisen first in the Middle East around 10,000 BC. By about 7000 BC, European farmers were beginning to clear the land and raise crops that could be stored throughout the year. Long-term food storage made it possible for relatively large numbers of people to remain permanently in one place rather than embarking on seasonal migrations in search of sustenance. With this change came the formation of a ranked society of chieftains, merchants, artisans, and farmers.

After 4000 BC, when the appearance of the plow led to agriculture on a larger scale, farming and animal-raising communities came to dominate much of Europe. Throughout the centuries that followed, the Continent was transformed by the introduction of copper, which allowed for more flexibility in toolmaking and in ornamentation, and the appearance of wheeled carts, which made it possible to transport bulk goods over long distances.

In addition, it was during this time that the peoples of Europe began erecting their most spectacular and durable monuments, the megaliths, or "great stones." Stonehenge, which still broods over southern England's barren Salisbury Plain, remains one of the most imposing. By about 3000 BC, tens of thousands of megaliths had been raised along the Atlantic and North Sea coasts, ranging from modern-day Spain to Scandinavia. No matter what their other achievements, though, Europeans never lost sight of the importance of farming, as indicated by the sickle-bearing god figure above, dating from the mid-third millennium BC.

BRONZE AGE
2000-800 BC

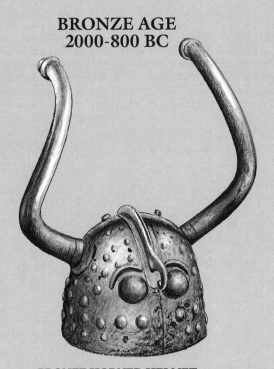

BRONZE HORNED HELMET

IRON AGE
800 BC-0

HORSE-HARNESS PLAQUE

Around 2000 BC, at the same time that Europe's first urban civilizations were emerging along the shores of the Aegean Sea, metallurgists discovered that an alloy of tin and copper would produce bronze, a metal that was harder than tin or copper and that could be fashioned into sharp-edged implements and cast into large and intricate decorative objects. By 1800 BC, thriving centers of mining, metalworking, and trade had arisen in central Europe. Bronze jewelry, weaponry, and domestic wares were dispersed throughout much of the Continent, and such articles were frequently entombed with the bodies of high-ranking individuals. These grave sites, along with other hoards of bronze goods, some of which may have been deposited as offerings to the gods, have provided a wealth of knowledge about life in these prehistoric times.

Central to the rise of metallurgy in Europe was the so-called Únětice culture, which rose in east-central Europe. From this key geographical location, the Únětice people exploited and controlled Balkan and Alpine copper deposits, the tin deposits of Bohemia, and the trade routes that brought goods from the Mediterranean into northern Europe.

By the middle of the second millennium BC, bronzeworking had reached Scandinavia. A spectacular development in metalworking resulted, as Scandinavian artisans consumed huge volumes of imported bronze in turning out delicately crafted objects, such as the ceremonial horned helmet shown above. At the same time, though, armorers throughout Europe were casting bronze into sword blades and battle-axes. These were wielded to chilling effect by a depredating warrior class that—along with the fortified settlements built for protection against such raiders—became a symbol of the age.

Ironworking, first introduced into central Europe in about 800 BC, was accompanied by the rise of an economically well developed people whose descendants are known as the Celts. Their culture first bloomed during the Hallstatt era, so called for the village in Austria where an expansive Early Iron Age cemetery and salt-mining center was discovered. For several centuries, as ironworking spread throughout the Continent, the Hallstatt culture went with it, carried even as far as the British Isles by waves of Iron Age migrants.

Like the Bronze Age elite before them, a warrior class grew rich through domination of trade with the Mediterranean world to the south. These warlords ruled from hilltop strongholds sited strategically along roads and waterways. Their power waned somewhat in the fifth century BC, possibly because of disruptions in trade, but by 450 BC, commerce had revived and new centers of Celtic civilization were arising. Bent on plunder or conquest, armed Celtic raiders, often trailed by settlers, ranged beyond their familiar territories. In about 400 BC, they crossed the Alps into northern Italy; in 391 BC, Celtic warriors pushed south to sack the great city of Rome.

The third century BC saw Celtic culture at its height, holding sway from Ireland to Italy, from the Iberian Peninsula westward to modern Ukraine. But a resurgent Rome soon began pushing into the Celts' vast domains. By the end of the second century BC, the Romans had taken over northern Italy and parts of southern France. Rome's legions continued to press northward until the British Isles remained the last redoubt of a once-dominant Celtic culture. There, artisans continued working in the Celtic tradition to craft such objects as the first century AD bronze horse-harness plaque seen above.

ACKNOWLEDGMENTS

The editors wish to thank the following individuals and institutions for their valuable assistance in the preparation of this volume:

Emmanuel Anati, Centro Camuno di Studi Preistorici, Capo di Ponte, Brescia, Italy; David Anthony, Anthropology Department, Hartwick College, Oneonta, New York; Martin Bates, Geoarcheological Service, Institute of Archeology, University of London; Paul Bennett, The Dover Bronze Age Trust, Canterbury, Kent, England; Louis Bonnamour, Conservateur, Musée Denon, Chalons-sur-Saone, France; Aimé Boquet, Président, Centre de Documentation de la Préhistoire Alpine, Grenoble; Grazia-Maria Bulgarelli, Soprintendenza per il Museo Preistorico ed Etnografico Pigorini, Rome; Henri Cosquer, Cassis, France; Jean Courtin, Directeur de Recherche au C.N.R.S., Marseilles; The Cultural Relics Bureau, Foreign Affairs Division, Beijing; Peter Dunn, English Heritage, London; Markus Egg, Römisch-Germanisches Zentralmuseum, Mainz; Michel Egloff,

Conservateur, Musée Cantonal d'Archéologie, Neuchâtel, Switzerland; Walter Fasnacht, Curator, Swiss National Museum, Zurich; Mechthild Freudenberg, Archäologisches Landesmuseum, Schloss Gottdorf, Schleswig, Germany; Ervin Garrison, Department of Anthropology, University of Georgia, Athens, Georgia; Irene Good, University of Pennsylvania, Philadelphia; Tancred Gouder, National Museum of Archeology, La Valletta, Malta; Friedrich-Wilhelm von Hase, Römisch-Germanisches Zentralmuseum, Mainz; Elena Izbitzer, New York, New York; Hans-Eckart Joachim, Rheinisches Landesmuseum, Bonn; Dolkun Kamberi, Columbia University, New York, New York; Flemming Kaul, The National Museum of Denmark, Copenhagen; Heidi Klein, Bildarchiv Preussischer Kulturbesitz, Berlin; Marie-Jeanne Lambert, Conservateur des Musées du Jura, Conservateur du Musée d'Archéologie de Lons-le-Saunier, Lons-le-Saunier, France; Giovanni Lattanzi, Giuli(ana, Teramo, Italy; Franco Marzatico, Ufficio

Beni Archeologici, Provincia Autonoma di Trento, Trento, Italy; Museo Archeologico Nazionale, Cagliari, Sardinia, Italy; Dieter zur Nedden, Radiologische Abteilung, Universitätsklinik, Innsbruck; Stuart Needham, British Museum, London; Pierre Petrequin, Directeur de Recherche au C.N.R.S., Besançon, France; Barbara A. Purdy, Professor Emerita, University of Florida, Gainesville, Florida; Denis Ramseyer, Conservateur, Service Archéologique Cantonal, Fribourg, Switzerland; Alain Roussot, Conservateur, Musée d'Aquitaine, Bordeaux; Ulrich Ruoff, Büro für Archäologie, Zurich; Helmut Schlichterle, Landesdenkmalamt Baden-Württemberg, Archäologische Denkmalpflege, Hemmenhofen, Germany; Horst Seidler, Institut für Humanbiologie und Anthropologie, Universität, Vienna; Konrad Spindler, Institut für Vor-und Anthropologie, Universitäat, Innsbruck; Françoise Vin, Centre de Documentation de la Préhistoire Alpine, Grenoble; Johannes Wiemann, Württembergisches Landesmuseum, Stuttgart.

PICTURE CREDITS

Camp and Associates. 63: Erich Lessing/Art Resource. 64: Gianni Dagli Orti, Paris. 66, 67: Charles Tait, Orkney. 68: © Adam Woolfitt/Robert Harding Picture Library, London. 69: © Michael J. O'Kelly. 70: Photograph Edwin Smith, Saffron Walden, Essex; photograph J. P. F. Stone Archive/ Wessex Archeology, © English Heritage. 71: Artwork by John Drummond, Time-Life staff. 73: Rosgarten Museum Konstanz, painting by Carl von Häberlin. 75: Baugeschichtliches Archiv/Büro für Archäologie. 76: J. M. Coles, Devon. 77: Büro für Archäologie; Landesdenkmalamt Baden-Württemberg, Archäologische Denkmalpflege, Arbeitsstelle Hemmenhofen. 78, 79: The Canterbury Archeological Trust, Kent, England. 80: The National Museum of Denmark, Copenhagen—Swiss National Museum. 81: A. Bocquet; photograph Rensi-Gino Zullo—Claude Huyghens/Françoise Danrigal; photograph Rensi-Gino Zullo. 82: Claude Huyghens/Françoise Danrigal (4) —J. M. Coles, Devon—Landesdenkmalamt Baden-Württemberg, Archäologische Denkmalpflege, Arbeitsstelle Hemmenhofen. 83: Swiss Historical Museum—Landesdenkmalamt Baden-Württemberg, Archäologische Denkmalpflege, Arbeitsstelle Hemmenhofen; Claude Huyghens/Françoise Danrigal. 84: Kenneth Garrett. 86: Dr. Gerlinde Haid, Sölden. 87: Dieter zur Nedden, Abteilung für Röntgendiagnostik und Computertomographie, Universität Innsbruck. 90: Dyrek Museum Archeologicznego, Poznan. 92: Copyright 1994 by WARA, Centro Camuno di Studi Preistorici, 25044 Capo di Ponte, Italy. 94: Claude Huyghens/ Françoise Danrigal. 95: Beat Arnold, Paris—Ufficio Beni Archeologici della Provincia Autonoma di Trento. 96: Photograph R. M. N., Paris. 97: © The British Museum, London. 99: J. M. Labat. 101: Georg Gerster/ Comstock. 102: Lee Boltin/Boltin Picture Library. 103: C. M. Dixon, Canterbury, Kent, England. 104: Erich Lessing/Art Resource. 105: Varna Eneolithic Necropolis. 106, 107: © The British Museum, London. 109: Landesamt für Archäologische Denkmalplege Sachsen-Anhalt, Landesmuseum für Vorgeschichte, Halle/photograph by L. Bieler. 110, 111: Pytheas, Vienna. 113-119: Background Tappeiner, Lana, Italy. 113: Photograph Herbert Maurer, Universität Innsbruck. 114, 115: Julia Ribbeck and Hartmut Schmidt, Römisch-Germanisches Zentralmuseum, Mainz/Christin Beeck; Sygma— photograph Herbert Maurer, Universität Innsbruck. 116: Kenneth Garrett—Julia Ribbeck and Hartmut Schmidt, Römisch-Germanisches Zentralmuseum, Mainz. 117-119: Julia Ribbeck and Hartmut Schmidt, Römisch-Germanisches Zentralmuseum, Mainz. 120-127: The National Museum of Denmark, Copenhagen. 128: Bildarchiv Preussischer Kulturbe- sitz, Berlin. 131: Photograph Schweiz, Landesmuseum. 133: Bildarchiv Preussischer Kulturbesitz, photograph by Jürgen Liepe, Berlin. 135: The National Museum of Denmark, Copenhagen. 136: Antikvarisk-topografiska arckivet, Stockholm, Sweden. 137, 138: from *The Chariot of the Sun and other Rites and Symbols of the Nothern Bronze Age* by Peter Gelling and Hilda Roderick Ellis Davidson, J. M. Dent & Son, London 1969. 139: Antikvarisk-topografiska arckivet, Stockholm, Sweden. 141: Drawing by Peter Dunn, © English Heritage Picture Library, London. 143: C. M. Dixon, Canterbury, Kent, England. 144: The National Museum of Denmark, Copenhagen—© The British Museum, London. 145: Photograph R. M. N., Paris—Elena Munerati, Trento/ courtesy Castello del Buonconsiglio, Monumenti e Collezioni Provinciali, Trento; Gianni Dagli Orti, Paris. 146: The National Museum of Denmark, Copenhagen. 147: Prähistorische Staatssammlung, Museum für Vor-und Frühgeschichte. 149, 150: Jeffery Newbury/Discover mummies of Xinjiang. 151: Map by John Drummond, Time-Life staff; Dr. Victor Mair (2). 152: Cultural Relics Publishing House, Beijing—Irene Good. 153: Dr. Victor Mair (2)—Cultural Relics Publishing House, Beijing. 154, 155: Dr. Dulkan Kamberi, Columbia University. 156, 157: Jeffery Newbury/Discover mummies of Xinjiang. 158, 159: Artwork by Paul Breeden.

BIBLIOGRAPHY

BOOKS

Anati, Emmanuel:
I Camuni alle Radici della Civiltà Europea. Milan: Jaca Book, 1982.
Val Camonica Rock Art: A New History for Europe. Val Camonica, Italy: Edizioni del Centro, 1994.

Barfield, Lawrence. *Northern Italy before Rome*. New York: Praeger Publishers, 1972.

Barker, Graeme. *Prehistoric Farming in Europe*. Cambridge: Cambridge University Press, 1985.

Barnatt, John. *Prehistoric Cornwall: The Ceremonial Monuments*. Wellingborough, Northamptonshire, England: Turnstone Press, 1982.

Bradley, Richard. *The Passage of Arms: An Archaeological Analysis of Prehistoric Hoards and Votive Deposits*. New York: Cambridge University Press, 1990.

Breeden, Robert L., ed. *Mysteries of the Ancient World*. Washington, D.C.: The National Geographic Society, 1979.

Brennan, Martin. *The Boyne Valley Vision*. Portlaoise, Ireland: The Dolmen Press, 1980.

Briard, Jacques. *The Bronze Age in Barbarian Europe*. Translated by Mary Turton. London: Routledge and Kegan Paul, 1979.

Burenhult, Göran, ed. *People of the Stone Age: Hunter-Gatherers and*

Early Farmers (The Illustrated History of Humankind series). New South Wales, Australia: Weldon Owen, 1993.

Burl, Aubrey. *Prehistoric Avebury*. New Haven, Connecticut: Yale University Press, 1979.

Chippindale, Christopher. *Stonehenge Complete*. Ithaca, New York: Cornell University Press, 1983.

Clark, J. G. D. *Prehistoric Europe: The Economic Basis*. New York: Philosophical Library, 1952.

Clottes, Jean, and Jean Courtin. *Grotte Cosquer*. Paris: Éditions du Seuil, 1994.

Coles, Bryony, and John Coles:
People of the Wetlands: Bogs, Bodies, and Lake-Dwellers. New York: Thames and Hudson, 1989.
Sweet Track to Glastonbury: The Somerset Levels in Prehistory. New York: Thames and Hudson, 1986.

Coles, J. M., and A. F. Harding. *The Bronze Age in Europe*. New York: St. Martin's Press, 1979.

Coles, John M., and Andrew J. Lawson, eds. *European Wetlands in Prehistory*. Oxford: Clarendon Press, 1987.

Constable, George, and the Editors of Time-Life Books. *The Neanderthals* (The Emergence of Man series). New York: Time-Life Books, 1973.

Cosquer, Henri. *La Grotte Cosquer*. Paris: Solar, 1992.

Cunliffe, Barry, ed. *The Oxford Illustrated Prehistory of Europe*. Oxford: Oxford University Press, 1994.

Daniel, Glyn, ed. *A Short History of Archaeology*. London: Thames and Hudson, 1981.

Dyer, James. *Ancient Britain*. Philadelphia: University of Pennsylvania Press, 1990.

The Editors of Time-Life Books. *Feats and Wisdom of the Ancients* (Library of Curious and Unusual Facts series). Alexandria, Virginia: Time-Life Books, 1990.

Gelling, Peter, and Hilda Ellis Davidson. *The Chariot of the Sun and Other Rites and Symbols of the Northern Bronze Age*. New York: Frederick A. Praeger, 1969.

Gimbutas, Marija:
Bronze Age Cultures in Central and Eastern Europe. The Hague: Mouton & Co., 1965.

The Civilization of the Goddess. Edited by Joan Marler. New York: HarperCollins, 1991.
The Goddesses and Gods of Old Europe: 6500-3500 BC. Berkeley: University of California Press, 1982.
The Language of the Goddess. New York: Harper & Row, 1989.

Glob, P. V. *The Mound People: Danish Bronze Age Man Preserved*. Translated by Joan Bulman. Ithaca, New York: Cornell University Press, 1974.

Hårdh, Birgitta, et al. *Trade and Exchange in Prehistory*. Lund, Sweden: Lunds Universitets, 1988.

Harding, Dennis. *The Making of the Past: Prehistoric Europe*. Oxford: Elsevier-Phaidon, 1978.

Harpur, James, and Jennifer Westwood. *The Atlas of Legendary Places*. New York: Weidenfeld & Nicolson, 1989.

Hvass, Steen, and Birger Storgaard, eds. *Digging into the Past: 25 Years of Archaeology in Denmark*. Translated by John Hines and Joan F. Davidson. Copenhagen: The Royal Society of Northern Antiquaries, 1993.

Jensen, Jørgen:
Guides to the National Museum: Prehistory of Denmark. Translated by Joan F. Davidson. Copenhagen: The National Museum, 1993.
The Prehistory of Denmark. London: Methuen & Co., 1982.

Joussaume, Roger. *Dolmens for the Dead: Megalith-Building throughout the World*. Translated by Anne and Christopher Chippindale. Ithaca, New York: Cornell University Press, 1988.

Longworth, I. H. *Prehistoric Britain*. London: British Museum Publications, 1985.

McIntosh, Jane. *The Practical Archaeologist: How We Know What We Know about the Past*. New York: Facts on File Publications, 1986.

Merriman, Nick. *Early Humans*. London: Dorling Kindersley, 1989.

Milisauskas, Sarunas. *European Prehistory*. New York: Academic Press, 1978.

Mohen, Jean-Pierre. *The World of Megaliths*. New York: Facts on File Publications, 1989.

Morrison, H. Robert. *Megaliths: Europe's Silent Stones*. Washington, D.C.: National Geographic Society

Special Publications, 1979.

Muir, Richard. *The Stones of Britain*. London: Michael Joseph, 1986.

O'Kelly, Michael J. *Newgrange: Archaeology, Art, and Legend*. London: Thames and Hudson, 1982.

Parker, Geoffrey, ed. *The World: An Illustrated History*. London: Times Books, 1986.

Past Worlds: The Times Atlas of Archaeology. Maplewood, New Jersey: Hammond, 1988.

Pearson, Michael Parker. *Book of Bronze Age Britain* (English Heritage series). London: B. T. Batsford, 1993.

Perini, Renato. *Scavi Archeologici nella Zona Palafitticola di Fiavé-Carera*, Vol. 1. Trento, Italy: Servizio Beni Culturali, 1984.

Phillips, Patricia. *The Prehistory of Europe*. Bloomington: Indiana University Press, 1980.

Piggott, Stuart. *The Earliest Wheeled Transport from the Atlantic Coast to the Caspian Sea*. New York: Thames and Hudson, 1983.

Pryor, Francis. *Book of Flag Fen: Prehistoric Fenland Centre* (English Heritage series). London: B. T. Batsford, 1991.

Purdy, Barbara A., ed. *Wet Site Archaeology*. Caldwell, New Jersey: Telford Press, 1988.

Quest for the Past. Pleasantville, New York: The Reader's Digest Association, 1984.

Renfrew, Colin. *Before Civilization: The Radiocarbon Revolution and Prehistoric Europe*. New York: Alfred A. Knopf, 1973.

Richards, Julian. *Book of Stonehenge* (English Heritage series). London: B. T. Batsford, 1991.

Rying, Bent. *Denmark: Danish in the South and the North*, Vol. 1. Copenhagen: Royal Danish Ministry of Foreign Affairs, 1981.

Sandars, N. K. *Prehistoric Art in Europe*. Harmondsworth, Middlesex, England: Penguin Books, 1985.

Sauter, Marc R. *Switzerland: From Earliest Times to the Roman Conquest*. Boulder, Colorado: Westview Press, 1976.

Scarre, Chris, ed. *Timelines of the Ancient World*. London: Dorling Kindersley, 1993.

Service, Alastair, and Jean Bradbery. *A Guide to the Megaliths of Europe*.

London: George Weidenfeld and Nicolson, 1979.

Spindler, Konrad. *The Man in the Ice.* Translated by Ewald Osers. London: Weidenfeld and Nicolson, 1994.

Stonehouse, Bernard. *Britain from the Air.* New York: Crown, 1982.

Stringer, Christopher, and Clive Gamble. *In Search of the Neanderthals: Solving the Puzzle of Human Origins.* New York: Thames and Hudson, 1993.

Trinkaus, Erik, and Pat Shipman. *The Neandertals: Changing the Image of Mankind.* New York: Alfred A. Knopf, 1992.

von Reden, Sibylle. *Die Megalith-Kulturen.* Cologne: DuMont Buchverlag, 1978.

Wernick, Robert, and the Editors of Time-Life Books. *The Monument Builders* (The Emergence of Man series). Alexandria, Virginia: Time-Life Books, 1979.

White, Randall. *Dark Caves, Bright Visions: Life in Ice Age Europe.* New York: The American Museum of Natural History, 1986.

Whittle, Alasdair. *Neolithic Europe: A Survey.* Cambridge: Cambridge University Press, 1985.

PERIODICALS

Bennike, Pia, and Klaus Ebbesen. "The Bog Find from Sigersdal." *Journal of Danish Archaeology,* Vol. 5, 1986.

Clottes, Jean, and Jean Courtin. "Neptune's Ice Age Gallery." *Natural History,* April 1993.

Clottes, Jean, et al. "Cosquer Cave on Cape Morgiou." *Antiquity,* September 1992.

Daniel, Glyn. "Megalithic Monuments." *Scientific American,* July 1980.

"The Discovery of a Bronze Age Timber Boat." *Current Archaeology 133,* March/April 1993.

Gimbutas, Marija:
"Gold Treasure at Varna." *Archaeology,* January 1977.
"Varna: A Sensationally Rich Cemetery of the Karanovo Civilization about 4500 B.C." *Expedition,* Summer 1977.

Gladkih, Mikhail I., Ninelj L. Kornietz, and Olga Soffer. "Mammoth-Bone Dwellings on the Russian Plain." *Scientific American,* November 1984.

"The Hand of Time." *Life,* December 1991.

Jovanović, Borislav. "The Origins of Copper Mining in Europe." *Scientific American,* May 1980.

Kamberi, Dolkun. "The Three Thousand Year Old Chärchän Man Preserved at Zaghunluq." In *Sino-Platonic Papers,* University of Pennsylvania, January 1994.

Keys, David. "Computer Reveals Face of Man Dead for 5,000 Years." *The Independent,* London: August 8, 1994.

Lewin, Roger. "Paleolithic Paint Job." *Discover,* July 1993.

Lumley, Henry de . "A Paleolithic Camp at Nice." *Scientific American,* May 1989.

Mair, Victor. "A Study of the Genetic Composition of Ancient Desiccated Corpses from Xinjiang (Sinkiang), China." *Early China News,* Fall 1993.

Milisauskas, Sarunas, and Janusz Kruk. "Neolithic Economy in Central Europe." *Journal of World Prehistory,* 1989.

"The Peopling of the Earth." *National Geographic,* October 1988.

Piggott, Stuart. "Timber Circles: A Re-Examination." *The Archaeological Journal,* July 1940.

"Présentation des Collections du Musée de Lons-le-Saunier, No. 1: Néolithique Chalain-Clairvaux Fouilles Anciennes." Lons-le-Saunier: Musées de France, October 1985.

Renfrew, Colin:
"Bulgaria's Ancient Treasures." *National Geographic,* July 1980.
"The Social Archaeology of Megalithic Monuments." *Scientific American,* November 1983.

Roberts, David:
"The Ice Man: Lone Voyager from the Copper Age." *National Geographic,* June 1993.
"Tantalizing to Scholars and Tourists, Carnac's Megaliths Remain an Enigma." *Smithsonian,* September 1989.

Todorowa, Henrieta. "Kultszene und Hausmodell aus Ovcarovo, Bez Targoviste." *Thracia III,* Academia Litterarum Bulgarica, 1974.

Wainwright, Geoffrey. "Woodhenges." *Scientific American,* November 1970.

Wilford, John Noble. "Iceman's Stone Age Outfit Offers Clues to a Culture." *The New York Times,* June 21, 1994.

OTHER SOURCES

"The Alpine Iceman: Hunter, Toolmaker, Cook." *National Geographic,* September 1994.

Bulletin de la Société Préhistorique Française, Vol. 89, No. 4, 1992.

Fedele, Francesco, ed. "L'Altopiano di Ossimo-Borno nella Preistoria. Ricerche 1988-1990." In *Studi Camuni,* Vol. 10. Capo di Ponte, Italy: Edizione del Centro, 1990.

"The Loulan Kingdom and the Eternal Beauty." Catalogue. Research Center for the Culture and Archaeology of Sinkiang, 1992.

Milisauskas, Sarunas, and Janusz Kruk:
"Economy, Migration, Settlement Organization, and Warfare during the Late Neolithic in Southeastern Poland." In *Germania,* Vol. 67, 1989.
"Settlement Organization and the Appearance of Low Level Hierarchical Societies during the Neolithic in the Bronocice Microregion, Southeastern Poland." In *Germania,* Vol. 62, 1984.

Parfitt, Keith, and Valerie Fenwick. "The Rescue of Dover's Bronze Age Boat." In *A Spirit of Enquiry.* London: National Maritime Museum, 1993.

Renfrew, Colin. "Problems in European Prehistory." Papers. New York: Cambridge University Press, 1979.

Wainwright, G. J., and I. H. Longworth. "Durrington Walls: Excavations, 1966-1968." Report. London: The Society of Antiquaries, 1971.

J

K

L

M

N

O

P

Paladru, Lake: 72; Neolithic knives recovered from, *81*

Paleolithic Age: bone implements, *24, 25, 26, 27, 158;* burials, 123; carved rock ball, *49;* chronology of, 14-15; reconstructions of European life during, *49;* stone artifacts from, 14-16, 18-19; subperiods of, 16; tooth-and-shell necklace, *28-29*

Paris Universal Exhibition: 31

Paulik, Josef: excavations at Ockov, 142-143

Peabody Museum: 31

Peacock Lady (mummy): *149*

Peacock River: 149

Pergine Valsugana, Italy: bronze greave found at, *145*

Phoenicians: 62

Piette, Édouard: 31

Piltdown man: 18-19; tooth of, *18*

Pirpamer, Markus: 86

Pomona, Scotland: Neolithic village on, *66-67*

Portal dolmens: *42-43*

Pottery: 54-56, 66; Beaker ware, 71, 103, *106,* 107, 108; Bronocice Vessel, *52;* cardial ware, 54; cord-decorated, 103; Corded Ware, 108; cups in form of wheeled carts, *53;* Linear Pottery, 54-57; Vinča, 54, 100

Poulnabrone Dolmen: *38-39*

Prescelly Mountains: source of Stonehenge's bluestones, 67

Proto-Celts: 141

Pryor, Francis: excavations at Flag Fen, 136-137

Q

Qaradöwä, China: fabric recovered near, *152;* mummy found at, *150;* prehistoric cemetery at, 150, *151;* wheel uncovered at, *153*

Qomul, China: 150, 152

R

Ramisch-Germanisches Zentralmuseum (Mainz): 116

Reinerth, Hans: 146-147

Religion: ceremonial centers, 60; fertility idol, *64;* Great Goddess, 62; images of sun deities, 98, 132-134, *135;* indications of, 23; ritual activities, 135, *139;* ritual figurines, *55;* ritual

sacrifice, 46, 111, 134, 143; shamanism, 34; sickle-bearing god-figure, *158;* statuary, *44;* Vinča mother-goddess and altar, 100; votive offerings, 96, 121, 129, 132, 137, *146*

Remedello, Italy: artifacts excavated from ancient cemetery at, 88; statue menhirs found at, 88

Remedello culture: 88-89

Renfrew, Colin: 58-59, 102, 108-109

Ribbeck, Julia: 116

Ridgeway: 140

Rillaton Barrow, Cornwall, England: 103; gold drinking cup found in, *102*

Roberts, Mark B.: and Boxgrove fossil, 9, 14

"Roger." *See* Boxgrove fossil

Romans: 159

Rudna Glava, Serbia: copper mines at, 100, 102

Russia: excavation of buried wagon site, *53*

S

Saka: 152, 154

Salisbury Cathedral: 63

Salisbury Plain: megaliths on, *37,* 60, 68, 74

Salt: trade in, 139

Sardinia: idol found at, *64;* warrior statuette found on, *145*

Sarich, Vincent: DNA research by, 25

Sarn-y-bryn-caled: excavation at, 45-46, 47

Sautuola, Marcellino de: discovery of Altamira cave art, 31-32

Sautuola, Maria de: 31-32

Scandinavia: burials in, 134, 135, *137;* hunting culture in, 130; metalworking in, 130Ÿ; skulls found in, *47, 56, 122, 123*

Scythians: 152, 154

Senorbi, Sardinia: idol found at, *64*

Severn River: 45, 67

Shennan, Stephen: 109

Ships: and cross-Channel trade, 110, 140; excavations of, *78, 79, 140;* Scandinavian, 134, *138*

Silbury Hill: *46*

Silk Road: 150

Simon, Helmut and Erika: 85-86

Single Grave people: 108

Sittard, Netherlands: Linear Pottery found at, 55

Skane, Sweden: rock carving found in, 135

Skara Brae: excavations at, *66-67*

Skrydstrup, Denmark: remains recovered from Bronze Age grave at, *122,* 127

Sorbonne: 96

Spindler, Konrad: and the Iceman, 87-91

Starčevo, Serbia: excavations at, 51, 54

Station Stones: 60

Stein, Netherlands: Linear Pottery found at, 55

Stone Age. *See* Paleolithic Age

Stonehenge: 9, *37,* 158; and astronomy, 64-65; components of, 60-61; construction of, 46-47, 65, 66, 67-69, *70, 71,* 72, 74; radiocarbon dating estimates, *49,* 66, 68; speculations on origin and function of, 47, 60, 63-64; subject of folklore and superstition, 60, 62-63; wooden precursors of, 45-47

Stonehenge II: 67

Stonehenge IIIa: 68-69

Stonehenge IIIc: 66, 70

Stukeley, William: 61, 62, 65-66

Sussex Archaeological Society: 19

Switzerland: beaded strings found in, *131*

T

Tacitus: 62

Taklamakan Desert: Indo-European mummies discovered in, *149-157*

Targovishte, Bulgaria: figurines found at, *55*

Tarim Basin: 149, 150

Teihard de Chardin, Pierre: 19

Tells: 49

Terra Amata, France: beach shelters used at, *17;* excavations at, *16*

Textiles: as evidence of European origins, 152; spindle and thread used for, *81*

Thom, Alexander: 64-65

Thomas, Herbert: 67

Thurnam, John: excavation of Beaker sites in England, 104-106, 107

Tombs: markings found in, 48

Trindhoj, Denmark: excavations at, 123-126

Trundholm solar chariot: 132-134, *135*

U

Ubeidiya, Israel: human fossils in, 17

Únetiče culture: metalworking skills of, 111-112, 159

Skara Brae

Callanish

TRUNDHOLM
CHARIOT

SKANE

Kivik

Newgrange

Egtved

Trundholm

NORTH SEA

Severn River

Flag Fen

Rhine River

Leubingen

Elbe River

Avebury
Stonehenge

Seine River

STONEHENGE

Únětice

BRITTANY
Carnac

Loire River

ATLANTIC OCEAN

*Lake of
Zurich*

Hallstatt

Lascaux Cave

A L P S

Altamira Cave

Val Camonica

P Y R E N E E S

VENUS OF WILLENDORF

SPANISH BEAKER POT

SARDINIA

MEDITERRANEAN SEA

SARDINIAN WARRIOR

MALTA